MY HOMETOWN CHICO *Another Look* 2

Marcia Myers Wilhite

Published by Marcia Myers Wilhite

Chico, California

Printed in China

ISBN: 0-9741048-1-7

MY HOMETOWN CHICO *Another Look* 2

Dedication

For Charlie—Again. More than ever.
Charlie II, Sarah, Jaime, Cameron, and Alec—Each of
you, in your unique and wonderful ways, inspire me
on a daily basis. I am blessed by your love.

Acknowledgements

Photographer, Ty Barbour—I am deeply thankful for your
enormous wisdom, support, and competence on this project. Our
friendship is one that I will always cherish. Taking time to run
around town photographing sites with me on your day off is a
deed that will never be forgotten. Your pictures are incredibly
insightful and filled with your obvious love of Chico.

Graphic Designer, Connie Nixon—Long, fast paced walks in the
park with our dogs, quick-witted conversations, and supportive
"emergency" phone calls are just a few things that come to mind.
Your art, talent, and understanding of the vision of this book
have been insurmountable.

Chico Enterprise Record, Publisher, Wolf Rosenberg, and Editor,
David Little—Thank you for helping to preserve valuable historic
data by letting me tap into your files for the creation of this
book. I am grateful for your support.

John and Penny Nopel—Thank you for welcoming me into your
home and caring about this project. I will always cherish your
friendship. I love you dearly.

My Dad, James Myers—For your open attitude that has taught
me to live life to it's fullest. For teaching me at an early age to
study the people and culture around me. For your cheery voice
at the other end of the telephone when I have spoken about this
project- I thank you with all my heart.

My Mother—An angel in heaven.

Downtown Merchants—For taking care of our beloved downtown
Chico. Without your unique and interesting businesses Chico
would not be what it is today.

Mr Kopy, SaraJean—For your understanding and care of the historic photographs and slides used for this project. Many thanks.

Christine LaPado—A true artist-writer and musician. Your
accounting of the music scene in Chico is superb.

Lori Silva—The laughter, the tears, triumphs, fears, and growing
closer through the years, ours is a friendship that will last forever.
I love you!

Heidi Genasci—The gift of your friendship is something that I
will always cherish. If I need a smile, belly laugh, or a vote of
confidence, I know that it will come from you! "When life gives
you a lemon have a lemon drop!"

"OUR PEOPLE do not understand even yet the *rich heritage* that is theirs"

—Theodore Roosevelt

Outdoor Pastimes of an American Hunter, 1905

Preface

While I was creating *My Hometown Chico—Another Look,* people would ask me, "What is your new book about?" Could there possibly be more to share about Chico since your last book?

I found that each time I would answer differently depending upon the page I was working on, or my mood at the moment. "This book is about … loving my hometown, living a passion, not giving up, memories almost forgotten, experiences, a town called Chico." I now realize that all these were true, each a vital ingredient of the story of *My Hometown Chico.*

Written and photographed from the truth of my heart, it is my hope to capture what is important to all who love Chico.

—Marcia Myers Wilhite

The

It has been my personal quest to photographically capture Chico, California. The pictures that fill these pages include those both historic and current. Chico is my hometown, and I have lived here my entire life. There are unique sites and wonderful stories that I want to share with my family and friends, as well as with those who have yet to experience Chico.

This captivating valley town, at the foothills of the Sierra Nevada Mountains, is a land that has both formed and reflects my own essence. Undoubtedly, it has touched many in the same way. For any native their thoughts on home are infused with a mixture of memory, myth, lore, and history, bound together in an erratic, subjective way. That mysterious mixture is why so much of this portrait is personal. Past and present are merged in its pages, as they are in my consciousness. But something else is in the mix too. Something magical. Something Chico.

It is certain that John Bidwell is the founding father of the city of Chico. In 1868, when Annie Bidwell arrived to her husband General John Bidwell's domain, she named his land, "The Wilderness." This great wilderness that we know and love is Chico. The wilderness that has become Chico has enriched many people spiritually, culturally, physically, and aesthetically. The city and surrounding area is an enduring resource that adds to the meaning and definition of our lives, nurtures our character, and sustains our beliefs.

Ty Barbour

"Little Chico" has grown into a much larger city than General John Bidwell had ever imagined. Change is inevitable. The expansion of Chico is obvious. Chico has matured into a thriving city that over 100,000 people call home. Nonetheless, Chico remains and always will be a magical place. Bidwell Park, the university, and downtown are just a sample of what is esteemed by many. In various ways, the people of Chico express certain common characteristics and emotions. The forms and details are different for every generation and every group, but certain traits and common bonds of Chico and its people have been repeated over the years. An obvious constant is that the town offers a strong sense of community. This, coupled with countless altruistic individuals has helped to shape the area unlike no other. Learn the tale of my hometown because once you come to Chico, it becomes your home too, no matter where you were born. It is my hope to encapsulate with photographs and stories the true nature of My Hometown Chico.

Another Look

The

As early as 1843, Edward Farwell and William Dickey rode their horses into what we now know as Chico and noted the desirability of the region. Edward Farwell made claim to the territory of the south side of the creek, and William Dickey chose land on the north side. In order to officially claim ownership of the region, they returned to Sutter's Fort to prepare grant applications. It is then that they named their land "Arroyo Chico," or "Little Creek." The formal Spanish translation read "Rancho Del Arroyo Chico." The claim is founded on a Mexican grant to William Dickey, made November 18, 1844, by Manuel Micheltorena, then governor of California, and containing five leagues of land. In July of 1844, Edward Farwell and Thomas Fallon settled upon Farwell's Grant, just south of Big Chico Creek, thus making the first white settlement within what is now the city of Chico.

John Bidwell's flour mill was located across from Bidwell Mansion next to where Northern Star Mills is located today. The mill ground both Bidwell's wheat crop and that grown from fields he leased to local farmers. The flour was of exceptional quality and earned an international status. A separate dam and water flume were constructed to bring waterpower to the mill.

The *Bidwells*

General John Bidwell was impressed with the region as he traveled through on horseback in the spring of 1843. It was he who roughly mapped the area, giving many of the streams and landmarks their names.

Bidwell returned in late1847 and was here when Marshall discovered gold in January 1848. He built a small and crude cabin south of the present Chico area, just outside of the Farewell Grant. John Bidwell discovered gold on the Feather River shortly after Marshall's discovery at Bidwell's Bar on July 4, 1848. It is there that he established his second home in Butte County. After mining for some time he returned to Arroyo Chico in 1849 and purchased the Rancho Del Arroyo Chico Grant from William Dickey. He was then able to build his third home, a cabin on the present mansion grounds.

Chico ER

Circa 1940

The cabin which was built with logs, burned down in 1852. Soon after, he replaced it with a two-story adobe dwelling, which was in close proximity to the site that we know as Bidwell Mansion. Construction of the mansion, as we know it, started in 1865 and was completed in 1868, at a cost of $56,000.

Between the years of 1849 and 1860 there were no houses south of Chico Creek. All of the homes were on General Bidwell's premises, and situated north of the stream. Bidwell purchased all of the land on both sides of Big Chico Creek, and eventually owned about 26,000 acres, extending from the Sacramento River to the upper part of what now is Bidwell Park.

Nopel Collection

Gary Quiring

2

Ty Barbour

During this period Chico had communication by stage with Oroville and Marysville, and steamboat transportation along the Sacramento River. The California Steamboat Navigation Company maintained an almost daily service along the Sacramento River. At Bidwell's suggestion, a survey was made by J.S. Henning, Butte County Surveyor, of a portion of the Rancho, lying between Big Chico and Little Chico Creeks. Under Bidwell's direction, the town of Chico was laid out and the plot plan filed on December 5, 1860 with the county recorder.

In 1864 Chico had a population of five hundred. In the middle of the decade Oroville claimed the same number, and the rivalry between the two communities became obvious. As the wheat industry expanded, Chico occupied a place of increasing importance in the county.

As a wedding gift for his bride, John Bidwell purchased a square rosewood piano. Today, this piano remains in the parlor of Bidwell Mansion, exactly where Annie used to sit and play for special guests. The piano has been restored to the same beauty and tone as when featured in musical evenings over 100 years ago.

Nopel Collection

The City of Chico has grown to an approximately 29 square mile charter city of 71,317 with an urbanized unincorporated area immediately adjacent to it with an additional population of 30,638, making the total population of the Chico urban area 101,955. 3

Chico

Streets

CHERRY ST

HAZEL ST

IVY ST

CHESTNUT ST

ORANGE ST

Downtown Chico was still quite rural when this picture of Broadway was taken. (Circa 1900) The streets were yet to be paved; however, the business district's comparative prosperity gave promise to the city's future growth, which would eventually make it the largest, most metropolitan city in the county.

Nopel Collection

The core of the city streets in Chico was in place by the 1870s. Under John Bidwell's direction, the town was laid out and the plot plan filed with the county recorder on the morning of December 5, 1860. During the mid to late 1800s, buggies, wagons, pedestrians and equestrians traveled the Esplanade. Today, the historical Esplanade is still lined with gorgeous trees, which are especially magnificent during the fall each year.

Near Chico State campus are five streets which head west: Chestnut, Hazel, Ivy, Cherry, and Orange Streets-the first letters spelling C-H-I-C-O. Normal Street was named after the Chico Normal School, the predecessor of Chico State. John and Annie Bidwell once referred to the park (Bidwell Park) as "Vallombrosa." The street directly across from Bidwell Park was in turn named Vallombrosa. In 1937, after the filming of Robin Hood in Chico, North Ivy Street was changed to Warner Street to honor Warner Brothers, the motion picture company.

Ty Barbour

Circa 1895

O.H. REICHLING

Nopel Collection

Photos Circa 1890

5th & Ivy

Marcia Wilhite

Five and I seems to be the hottest spot for college kids to congregate and socialize or party on most any occasion, especially Thursday, Friday, and Saturday nights. It's common for the kids to pop into Riley's or maybe stop by a party or two that could be taking place at a nearby fraternity or sorority house. During Halloween and St. Patrick's Day, the four-corner stop has literally blocked traffic due to long lines of people who are socializing or waiting in line to enter Riley's. Many people have heard about the so-called "riot" that took place during Pioneer Week in 1987. This is where it happened.

The corner location is truly "Old Chico" as Chico Soda Works was located here during the late 1800s.

Warner Street used to be the south end of Ivy Street, it was renamed in 1938, in honor of the Warner Brothers' motion picture Robin Hood, which was filmed in Chico.

Chico ER

Circa 1960

Circa 1890

Average annual rainfall in Chico is 25.75 inches.

Then *and* *Now*

Circa 1904, swanky Studebaker carriages were sold by E.E. Canfield.

Nopel Collection

While much has changed, much has remained the same. Our streets still have many of the same landmarks and Chicoans still enjoy many of the same activities.

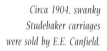

Chico ER

Pet Parade circa 1949—a Chico tradition that continues to this day.

Transportation in Chico circa 1890

Nopel Collection

Corner of 1st and Main circa 1949

Chico ER

Nopel Collection

Circa 1904, he should of stayed on the streets.

Women drivers in 1900

A circus arriving in Chico circa 1905.

3rd and Broadway circa 1890

Streetcar circa 1905

In 1864 Chico had a population of five hundred.   7

Good Old

Days

Nopel Collection

Bidwell School, circa 1890 was located where West Scaramento Avenue is today

Ty Barbour

The Bidwell Building was originally a two-story structure. The top story was removed after a fire destroyed two of the four walls. Some of the original windows are still in tact, and one wall is from the original structure. It has been home to Tres Hombres Long Bar & Grill since 1989. Many patrons have held a toast at the bar in honor of the great pioneer who once had his office in the same location—General John Bidwell.

Nopel Collection

Feed store on 7th Street circa 1910

Nopel Collection

Built in 1870, the Presbyterian Church originally stood on the corner of 4th and Broadway Streets.

Nopel Collection

Continental Nut

Continental Nut Company was described as the largest independent nut sheller and packer of edible, shelled nuts on the West Coast. Located on the Esplanade between East Tenth and Eleventh Avenues, the steel structure, governing an area of 45,000 square feet, was built in 1960 at a cost of $200,000.

Chico ER

Chico ER

Nopel Collection

The Bank of Chico, located on the corner of 2nd and Broadway circa 1900

Chico's first telephone company was operated by Gilly Barham.

Preview inside the old 2nd and Broadway Economy Store in 1910

Nopel Collection

Chico is 230 feet above sea level.　9

Wake up and smell the *Coffee*

Ty Barbour

During the 1940s, the stringencies of wartime economy were emphasized by lack of coffee thoughout the country, including in my hometown Chico. To combat the shortage, grocery stores carried "ersatz", an artificial coffee. "Jeep" was an interesting blend of rolled wheat flour, molasses, and corn oil, costing fifteen cents per pound. "Banner whole roasted cereal," was offered as a coffee extender, and was a value at four cents per pound.

Today, coffee houses are literally on every busy street corner in Chico. Rather than a regular "cup of joe" at the local diner, Chicoans are now sipping premium coffee made from freshly roasted exotic beans, in coffee houses which are architecturally pleasing to the eye, display art on the wall and often feature live music. In the 1990s people began slurping creative coffee concoctions made from a variety of flavored syrups and freshly whipped cream. The prices for coffee today have skyrocketed to one dollar and fifty cents per cup of coffee, and four dollars for a coffee drink.

Chico ER

Marcia Wilhite

Marcia Wilhite

1956 union picketers at The Broadway Coffee Shop.

It is the coffee ritual in the morning that many people enjoy. It's calming. It helps order the day. Coffee houses today are, to some degree, a supplement to the bar scenes of the past, only the socializing takes place in the morning.

Downtown

Downtown Events

Downtown Chico is the center of many community events, one of the most popular of which is Slice of Chico, held in conjunction with a sidewalk sale each July.

Taste of Chico

Twenty years ago people in Chico used to frequently say, "There's not enough good places to eat in Chico." Today, this is definitely not the case as Chico has many fine restaurants and eateries. Since 1989, once a year on a Sunday in September, the streets downtown are filled with people seizing the opportunity to sample Chico's varied culinary delights in the celebration known as a "Taste of Chico"

This young boy looks to be in absolute awe by the experience of speaking with Santa Claus. Children and their parents line up on 2nd Street during Christmas Preview each November to see the handsome Santa who sits in Magna Carta's festive store window.

Ty Barbour, ER

Chico has an average of 219 clear days in a typical year. 11

Some of
Our Uniquely, Chico

This is just a sampling of our wonderful merchants.

Collier Hardware—Syl Lucena Since 1963 (ownership)

Zucchini & Vine—Nancy Lindahl Since 1977

Grace Jr.—Grace Allread Since 1977- (downtown location)

Needham's Stained Glass Studio—Mick Needham Since 1971

Ty Barbour

Mountain Sports—Bruce Hart Since 1977

Nantucket—Rick and Nan Tofanelli Since 1975

Big Al's Drive In

Big Al's is a blast from the past, serving up "Happy Burgers" and "Triple Thick Shakes" for over fifty years. The original owner, Al Ragier, opened for business in 1950, and still lives in Chico. Located on "the strip" in Chico, Big Al's is a reminder for folks that lived life American Graffiti style, continuing to be a hangout for classic car and motorcycle buffs. But don't stay away if you're not the Fonz and Richie type. Their clientele is incredibly diverse; businessmen, students, farmers—afterall, who can resist a frosty cone?

What would Chico be like without downtown? It's hard to even imagine. Downtown is a lively, vital place filled with fun things to do and see. Chico's downtown merchants are the folks that have shaped downtown into what it is today. The merchants have put their heart and soul into their shops, many of them for over 25 years, creating the downtown that we know and love.

Ty Barbour

Betty's on Broadway—Summer Ballock
Since 1984

Nopel Collection

Warner Street Grocery

Gone are the days when you just can run down to the neighborhood market to pick up a carton of milk or a cube of butter. That is, unless you live near Warner Street Grocery. The doors first opened in 1937.

Most memorable, are the folks that took over in 1974. Frank and Martha White, brought a new meaning to the name family business. That is, if you include the countless people that adored and loved the White's as if they were their own family.

The floors are wooden and worn from age, and creak as you walk up the aisle. The front porch is an inviting spot to sit down and enjoy an ice cold soda and a freshly made sandwich.

Ty Barbour

Burger Hut

Ah ... the smell of a flame grilled burger, with golden fries, and a thick chocolate shake made from rich, creamy ice cream. Sound enticing? The Williams have been serving them up daily at Burger Hut on Nord Avenue since 1978. The author enjoyed this historically popular meal on one of her first dates in high school. Today, high school kids are still racing down west 1st Avenue during their lunch break to munch down a juicy burger. This place isn't just for kids. Locals, college students, and visitors alike scoff down Burger Hut burgers like there is no tomorrow.

Proprietors, Jim and Priscilla Williams arrived in Chico in 1968. Their three children; Christine, Erin, and Trevor were all born at Enloe Hospital, and raised in Chico. As young girls, Christine and Erin stood on a wooden box that their dad made for them in order to reach the counter to take orders from the customers. In the year 2000, the doors opened to the second Burger Hut establishment located on Forest Avenue. Now you can get a juicy burger on both sides of town in Chico.

Bird in Hand, the Malowney Family since 1981.

Oy Vey Café served Chicoans their first bagel in 1979.

13

Maisie Jane's California Sunshine Products

Maisie Jane Bertagna Hurtado grew up in an almond orchard in Chico. She is the fourth generation of a dedicated farming family. Her grandfather, the late Ben Bertagna, was not only highly regarded as an almond rancher, but as a pioneer in the almond industry for the Chico area. He was a kind-hearted man, who had a deep love for his family, agriculture, and the land he worked and lived on. It is obvious that his granddaughter, Maisie Jane, inherited more than a few of his qualities.

Ty Barbour

The amazing, Maisie Jane, "is" Chico. She learned early on how to help with the harvest of almonds, by driving the "sweeper". She drove the tractor on her family farm, moved pipe to water the trees, and hand hulled many almonds. At seventeen, she found an avenue to sell almonds keeping the pricing in the family's own hands.

This young woman has boundless energy. It all started in 1993, when Maisie Jane was a junior in high school and an active member in "Future Farmers of America." As an FFA project Maisie sold her entire flock of sheep to buy one ton of almonds.

In the fall of 1999, Maisie Jane was awarded the prestigious North American Collegiate Entrepreneur of the Year award, becoming the first woman ever to win the award. Not bad for a young businesswoman who literally built her company from the ground up six years previously.

Maisie Jane's processes a diverse line of over twenty different almond products using her family's and other local almond growers' crops. All of the products have been oven roasted and are all natural. In 2003, she introduced their new product line of Certified Organic Sliced Almonds. She sells to grocery stores nationwide; most of which are health food stores.

Working against the forces of time and a changing economy, Maisie Jane is constantly fighting to keep small family farms from becoming extinct. (Go Maisie!) Maisie Jane's California Sunshine Products currently sells 175 tons of almonds a year.

In 2004 the original N.T. Enloe Hospital site was lost to an intense electrical fire. For weeks local Chicoans passed by via car or by foot to see a piece of history. Photograph circa 1913.

All Historic Enloe photos courtesy of Enloe Hospital

Newton Thomas *Enloe* M.D.

Dr. Enloe is famous for "riding the flumes"—arriving in time to deliver a baby! Circa 1915

Located at 330 Flume Street, Dr. Newton Thomas Enloe opened his first official Chico hospital in 1913. Patient needs quickly outgrew the downtown location prompting Dr. Enloe to seek a large undeveloped site on the Esplanade to build a larger facility. The construction of the Esplanade Enloe Hospital took incredibly long to materialize, the new building, between 5th and 6th Avenue was completed in 1937, at a cost of approximately $75,000.

Enloe Medical Center has resided at its Esplanade location for nearly 70 years. Millions of people have held the hand of a loved one, said goodbye to a friend or family member, and greatest of all, welcomed new life into the world. The roots run incredibly deep.

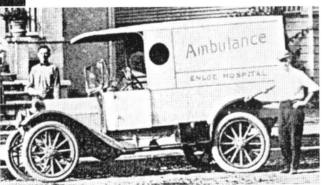

As the population of Chico has grown, so has the hospital. Enloe is a community-owned, nonprofit hospital that provides Chico and the North Valley with emergency medical service and hospital care. Enloe is renown for cutting edge medical techniques for cardiac care and cancer therapy. Over 2,000 people are on the payroll, making them one of Chico's largest employers.

Helicopter rescue in 2005.

Ty Barbour, ER

Early Ambulance Circa 1915

Chico's First Subdivision

Chapmantown

Many people wonder exactly where Chapmantown is, and why it got its name. First of all, in actuality, there are two Chapmantowns. One of the more interesting things is that the unincorporated area that many currently refer to as Chapmantown, that is between Boucher and the freeway, and Ninth and East 20th Streets, was a secondary development. It inherited its name from the original. No one ever definitely set the boundaries for the original Chapmantown or the area loosely called Chapmantown today.

The neighborhood we now commonly refer to as Chapmantown was originally ranch land in the late 19th century. During this same time, an ambitious man by the name of Augustus Chapman started Chico's first subdivision—Chapman's Addition. "Gus," a pioneer and businessman, purchased 160 acres of land with a plan to develop the open land into a comfortable, yet modest neighborhood for the young families of Chico.

For decades this subdivision was known as Chapmantown, and it was one of Chico's most valued neighborhoods. It extended from the south border of Little Chico Creek to 16th Street, and from Park Avenue to what is now Boucher Street.

Augustus H. Chapman was a highly successful businessman, pioneer, and in local status was nearly as prominent as John Bidwell. Chapman owned, at one time or another, two hotels, a large mercantile shop downtown, a major lumber company, a flourmill on Butte Creek, and Chico's gas and water companies. He was vice president of Chico's first bank, and was involved in various mining endeavors and road-building projects. He acted as a justice of the peace, a school and church trustee, and helped to establish a public library. Indeed, Augustus Chapman's list of accomplishments surely is impressive.

Little Chapman Mansion

A gentleman by the name of George Adams Smith laid the house's foundations in 1853. Mr. Smith was Butte County's first district attorney, as well as the first judge elected to office in the county. General John Bidwell valued him as a friend and his trusted personal attorney. It was John Bidwell who sold Smith this fine plot of land on the south side of Little Chico Creek, which was next to the rapidly increasing area that we know as Chico. Within weeks of the starting construction of the home, George Smith died at the age of forty-six from tuberculosis. The foundations of the house lay bare for six years.

In 1859 John B. "Doc" Smith acquired the acreage. No relation to the land's previous owner, John Smith was born in Ireland. "Doc" built the original core of the house, which still stands today. He raised cattle on the surrounding land until a severe drought throughout the valley ruined him financially. The land was foreclosed in 1862, and Smith died of unknown causes a mere eight weeks later.

Marcia Wilhite

Within four years the creditor of the land, James Tormey, sold the land to rancher John R. Woolen, who in turn sold it to Augustus H. Chapman in 1870. Chapman's name is widely recognized by Chicocans. It is his name that titles the Little Chapman Mansion, as well as the Chapmantown neighborhood.

The mansion is listed on the National Register of Historic Places, as well as the 1981 Chico Historic Resources Inventory. Chico State University Professor Michele Shover purchased the home in 1976. Shover teaches political philosophy and theory in Chico State's political science department.

Chapmantown School, Circa 1915

Since 1920, you can still get a

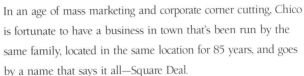

In an age of mass marketing and corporate corner cutting, Chico is fortunate to have a business in town that's been run by the same family, located in the same location for 85 years, and goes by a name that says it all—Square Deal.

Ennis, Lois, and Ruth circa 1925.

It all began in 1920. Ennis V. Rife started the business after he left a local bedding factory because the owner cheated his customers by replacing quality bedding material with cotton. The cotton would clump and compact into hard spots making for an uncomfortable mattress. The young and ambitious Rife, still in his teens, started a competing business that would provide customers with a "Square Deal." Hence was the birth of Square Deal Mattress Factory.

Ennis Rife circa 1920.

In the beginning it was just a two-person operation. Rife used an old hand picker to make fluff, which he would turn as his wife Leotta fed horse hair or kapok stuffing into mattress shells. They would then blow it into the ticks, which when full would be sewn up and then beaten down with sticks into familiar mattress shapes. When he had accumulated enough mattresses to sell, Ennis Rife would climb into his truck and go out on the road to sell mattresses all throughout northern California to Mom and Pop stores, hotels, and anyone else who would buy one. He loved meeting new people through his traveling and sales, while his wife, Leona, preferred to stay at home with their daughters, Lois and Ruth.

Leotta Rife, the founder's wife. Circa 1920

Circa 1925

Square Deal was able to survive the Depression. During World War II the business began to prosper due to large purchases from the United States Army and growth in the Chico area. It continued to grow post-war boom, adding along the way a reupholstering business and a rug cleaning service. By the 1950s it had outgrown its old building, and in 1957 they built a new one at the same Humboldt location.

Rife retired in 1982, leaving his store in the extremely capable hands of his daughter, Lois Lash, and his grandson, Richard Lash. It is Richard Lash that has taken leaps and bounds with the success of the business. A young, graduate, fresh out of Chico State, Lash had not originally intended on staying in town to run the family business.

Though once he took the reins of the company he was able to build a small empire. Lash immediately upgraded the equipment, hired more employees for production, and added "soft-top premium bedding" to keep up with the changing industry. Thus, enabling him to compete on a larger scale. Because Square Deal sells directly to the public, the high-end mattresses are priced at mid-range, therefore making high quality beds available to those who otherwise may not be able to purchase them. The company has also attracted many institutional customers. Numerous hotels, bed and breakfast houses, universities, and hospitals have also been able to experience the comfort of a Square Deal.

Richard Lash has been at the helm for over 20 years and is quite happy that his Grandpa persuaded him to stay in Chico. Lash's daughter works in the store, and is quite efficient at the family trade. His mother, Lois Lash, is still highly involved in the business. The store environment is friendly, honest, and continues to offer Chicoans a Square Deal.

A great place to *Visit*

Circa 1900

Nopel Collection

Nopel Collection

CHICO HOTEL

Nopel Collection

Circa 1939

Hotel Oaks

During the 1860s, the land where the Oaks Hotel was built was first used as a cattle corral. Located on the corner of 2nd and Salem, where a city parking lot is cemented today, the Oaks Hotel was in business for 48 years. Like many early buildings in Chico, the hotel was destroyed by fire.

Hotel Diamond—It is *Magical!*

Ty Barbour

On September 3, 1904, Mr. J.R. Adler opened Chico's Hotel Diamond on Fourth, between Broadway and Salem Streets. It was the finest hotel in town. Chico was a bustling small city with energetic entrepreneurs and dream seekers who were all hoping to strike it rich. Guests flocked from all over to stay in the Hotel Diamond's luxurious rooms and enjoy a meal in its fine restaurant.

The hotel became a hub for locals and visitors alike. It was such a success that in 1912, a few members of the community became suspicious and boasted that they thought the patrons of the hotel were having too much fun! It was then that the local Grand Jury opened an investigation of the hotel, placing the owner in an embarrassing and uncomfortable situation, to say the least. Just four years later, a disastrous fire swept through the building, forcing the popular Hotel Diamond to close its doors for the rest of the century. A small portion of the building was converted to warehouse and office space, but never used to its full potential.

What happened next is truly remarkable. In 2002, Wayne Cook, a local preservationist and developer purchased the dilapidated old building and began plans to restore it to its former grandiosity. If you were one of the lucky ones to tour the Hotel Diamond as it was under construction you were able to see and feel the magic of the building. The construction process has been incredibly intense, and like many large projects, has run far past any cost projections or scheduled opening date. The anticipation of it all makes the opening date even more exhilarating. As this book goes to print, the Hotel Diamond is within weeks of re-opening its doors to the public. The hotel has been the talk of town since they began construction three years ago. Chicoans anxiously await the grand opening of the spectacular Hotel Diamond.

The Chico Hotel

The Chico Hotel stood as a landmark in the late 1870s. The hotel was located on the corner of Second and Salem. Ira Wetherbee, one of the first firemen in Engine Co. 1, was the owner. Ironically, Ira's hotel held the dubious honor of being the first structure to receive water from Chico's new hand-pump fire engine when it was destroyed by fire in 1874. Although the original building was lost, its occupants all escaped with their belongings. Ira rebuilt his hotel in 1875.

Our *Veterans*

Ty Barbour. ER

Marcia Wilhite

Ty Barbour. ER

Veterans' Building

Located on the Esplanade, across from Chico High, the Veterans' Hall was built in 1927, at a cost of $90,000. It was the last of four built in Butte County during the 1920s. The others were located in Gridley, Biggs, and Paradise.

27ᵗʰ Training Squadron   Class 43-I   A.F.B.F.S.   June 2, 1943.

The citizens of Chico thank our veterans for their service and sacrifice. As time and generations pass it is sometimes forgotten that we enjoy the fruits of their efforts with the freedoms we enjoy. We salute you with our deepest appreciation.

In 1946, Veteran's housing was set up on the east side of Warner Street. Temporary quonset huts were installed.   21

The 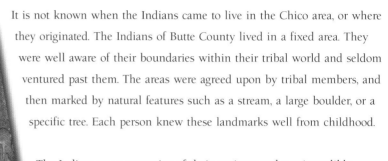 Maidu

It is not known when the Indians came to live in the Chico area, or where they originated. The Indians of Butte County lived in a fixed area. They were well aware of their boundaries within their tribal world and seldom ventured past them. The areas were agreed upon by tribal members, and then marked by natural features such as a stream, a large boulder, or a specific tree. Each person knew these landmarks well from childhood.

The Indians were protective of their territory and not incredibly tolerant of other tribes. Most people lived within a 15-mile distance and conversed with no more than one 100 people during their entire lives. Different dialects developed within what is now Butte County because of the isolated activities of the relatively small tribal groups. Travel of only a few miles from one Indian group to another would result in variation in language form. Indian villages were usually built near a large source of water, and it was common for them to choose a site on a knoll or promontory to avoid a surprising intruder.

Nopel Collection

Circa 1890

The first Indian inhabitants in Chico were of the northwestern Maidu group and were members of the Mechoopda tribe. They occupied the territory south of Big Chico Creek to the Bear River below what is now the Butte County line. The Mechoopda Indian tribe first lived on what later became Flume Street in east Chico. In 1849, John Bidwell moved the Mechoopda to a location approximately 300 yards southwest of his mansion. (Near the present Holt Hall at CSUC.) He did this to protect the Indians from destructive transient groups who sometimes traveled through the area.

Protected on Bidwell's land the Mechoopda thrived and subsequently integrated into the city of Chico.

Circa 1870

Nopel Collection

22

Edible Wild Plants in Butte County

Chico was known for its rich soil and bountiful plants. Wild game and fruiting plants were relatively easy for the Indians to acquire. The Maidu Indians who settled in Butte County made complete and extensive use of every useable plant for food, medicine, shelter, fuel, tools, fish and snare lines, weapons, basketry, and cooking utensils. The main plant food of the Maidu was acorns. The Maidu gathered acorns, then leached, and pounded the corn into meal for making gruel and soup. They also used acorns by mashing them and forming them into small flat cakes that were then baked. The Maidu were referred to as "Diggers" because they gathered by means of a digging stick, usually one meter in length, straight, and with the end hardened by fire. They would eat the roots raw, roasted, boiled and sometimes dried. Berries were mashed and baked into seeded cakes, or wrapped in leaves as a delicacy. They were gathered and dried to reserve for cold winter months when fruit was not in season.

Indians and early pioneers used greens and stalks from plants for salads, teas, and medicinal purposes. Many plants in the Butte County area were cooked and eaten raw. The pioneers discovered the importance of including greens in their diet as a prevention of scurvy. The use of local herbs was considered by mountain folks to be one of the most important constituents of nature's pharmaceutical supply.

Nopel Collection

Mechoopda Dance House Chico Rancheria 1898.

There are many wild food plants currently growing in Butte County that can be made into teas, or used as spices when cooking. Many of these plants are of the same variety that the Maidu once foraged upon hundreds of years ago. The plants may very well be growing in your backyard, and you can surely find them in the foothills, canyons, or nearby mountain range. Some people use them for home remedies for a cold or upset stomach; some may simply enjoy the natural beauty of the plant. Most importantly though, is that we are still able to take pleasure in the world that surrounds us and enjoy this incredible land that many are fortunate to call home—Chico.

Good Plants—Bad Plants

It is important to remember that there are extremely poisonous plants in Butte County that can be incredibly beautiful to look at, but should never be ingested. A few of the poisoness plants include: Buttercups, Bleeding Hearts, Corn Lilies, Jimson Weed, Lupine, Mistletoe, Periwinkle, Poison Oak, and Water Hemlock.

Author's note:

The author does not acknowledge the safe use of wild plants due to the unknown reaction that an individual may have to a particular plant.

"One man's food is another man's poison."

23

The Story of Ishi

The story of Ishi is one of the most improbable and fascinating episodes in the history of the American West. It just so happens, that this vital piece of history took place incredibly close to Chico, in the foothills of northern California. There is no single truth to Ishi's story, only fragments, gaps, and interpretations.

Ishi formulated the Yahi culture.

Pioneers massacred most of the Yahi tribe in the mid-nineteenth century. Ishi, the last Yahi, grew up in this time of turmoil and terror for the people of Native California. He was probably born sometime in the 1860s as the Civil War was in full rage back east. At that time, the Sacramento Valley, just below the ancestral Yahi foothills began to fill up with pioneers who came to California to find a better life, and claim California as their own.

At about the time of Yahi's birth, the Yahi went into hiding to avoid being captured. A half-century later, only four tribe members remained. Ishi and his companions hid out at a place they called Wowunupo Mu Tetna, or Grizzly Bear's hiding place. For nearly fifty years he hid in the foothills near Oroville, living in animal skins and hunting with a bow and arrow. The area was just a few miles from valley farmland; concealed beneath cliffs in a brushy area of Deer Creek Canyon.

Ishi was relatively primitive, using old traditions of Native America. From his elders, he had learned dozens of Yahi songs and the derivation of myths from his people. He harpooned salmon in nearby creeks, and cooked mush from acorns in finely woven handmade baskets. He sowed blankets out of animal hides from coyote, wildcat, and raccoons that he hunted. He lived in a hut made from brush and tree limbs with a doorway that was 33 inches high. To avoid starvation, Ishi and others were known to have stolen from nearby cabins where white men had established their homestead. Canned beans, bags of barley, and tins of biscuits became an integral part of Ishi's diet to survive. On occasion, he was known to poach sheep.

How was he caught?

After hiding out for decades in the hills above Oroville, Ishi was found hungry and half naked near this little town. Fortunately, the men who found him didn't kill him. It was decided that he should be shipped to San Francisco to be studied. In 1911, Ishi stood shoeless at the train station in Oroville as he waited for a train to take him to San Francisco. Today, the converted train station is occupied by The Depot Restaurant, which has been in business since 1977.

24

All Ishi photos: Nopel Collection

Twenty years after the Plains Wars, anthropologists proclaimed Ishi, the last of the Yahi tribe. It has been nearly a century since Ishi came down out of the mountains on a warm summer evening in search of food. He spoke no English at the time of his capture in Oroville. However, he somehow had learned a few Spanish words, which suggests that the Yahi had a more peaceful history of contact in the years before the birth of Ishi, passing down the language to the young boy.

Alfred Kroeber, a famous anthropologist, declared Ishi to be the most "uncontaminated" and "uncivilized" man in the world. After his capture, Ishi became somewhat of a celebrity, as Kroeber brought him to San Francisco where he showed him as an exhibit for a museum above Golden Gate Park. Each Sunday, thousands of visitors flocked to see "the wild man of deer creek." He was an oddity and extremely interesting to common society in the early twentieth-century. It was at the Museum of Anthropology in San Francisco, where Ishi spent the last five years of his life. He demonstrated bow and arrow making, achery, fire making, and other Yahi skills to guests at the museum. He worked as the Museum's janitor. In March 1916, Ishi died from tuberculosis. His death was devastating to Alfred Kroeber, the anthropologist who had spent years studying and understanding Ishi. Kroeber deeply missed the friendship that he had developed with Ishi.

Today, there are 107 small Indian reservations across the state. Living speakers of some 50 different native languages can be found even now. Ishi was the last Yahi and the state's most famous Indian.

The black boulders, powerful rapids, and deep emerald pools of Deer Creek is the territory that was once inhabited by Ishi and the last Yahi survivors.

In 1961 Chico State purchased 14 acres of land from Mechoopda Indians 25

Chinese

Chinese people entered California in the 1850s and 1860s. Life in the United States was a new beginning for the Chinese. China was being controlled by outside forces, which is why many Chinese made their way to Northern California. Some joined in on the rush to find gold in California. The Chinese that came to Butte County were primarily from Guangzhou, the capital of Guan don (Canton). It has been estimated that over 10,000 Chinese lived in Butte County by 1870, predominately the Oroville area. Along the Feather River in the southwest part of Oroville, the Chinese built a small town that was referred to as "Bagdad."

Chico had two China towns. "Old Town" was located on Flume between East Fifth and Sixth Streets. "New Town" was on Cherry Street between West Seventh and Ninth Streets. Old Town was established first, though both areas were built in the late 1800s. Each had its very elaborate Joss House or Temple.

During the early 1900s, most of the larger homes employed Chinese help; either cooks, gardeners, or both. They were treasured for their loyalty, honesty, and never-failing industry. Houseboys usually dressed in Mandarin jackets and commonly wore their hair in a queue, including a silk tassel braided at the end. It was their local Chinatowns that they might have word of their homeland by way of Sacramento or San Francisco.

The Chinese brought a cultural and exotic flare to little Chico. Colorful parades, firecrackers and dragon kites instilled a vibrant diversity to early Chico that was enjoyed by many residents.

There is another chapter of local history that many have actively questioned and researched, though there remains a deal of uncertainty as to the true facts. It concerns the anti-Chinese movement during the 1800s. Racial hatred was then, as it is now, incredibly unreasonable. During these years, there were many who felt that the Chinese were competing with the whites. The fact of the matter is, the Chinese at no time competed

Nopel Collection

with the white man during those days. It is more of the fact that the Chinese in Chico, as well as many other cities, did the work the white man would not do. It was the Chinese who planted the first orchard in Northern California. It was the Chinese who built the railroad into Oregon. The Chinese did not mix with the whites mostly because it was more comfortable for them to stay within their own culture.

Contrary to the belief of many locals, the Chinese did not build tunnels beneath the buildings in downtown Chico. It has been said that there were tunnels where they would "hide out" and use opium pipes. There is no evidence that there was any such thing. There simply were no tunnels. As for the use of opium, that is another matter. It has been documented that some of the Chinese did frequent "opium dens" in the Chinatowns, of early Chico.

Ty Barbour, ER

Old Humboldt Road Burn Dump

During the 1860s, John Bidwell built what is now known as Old Humboldt Road. Near Stilson Canyon in east Chico, Humboldt was one of the first roads to pass through the Sierra. Looking at it today, it doesn't appear that much has changed since those early pioneering days. The path climbs from the valley floor and disappears over a ridge into the foothills. Early settlers used this road to move freight and mail to and from mines in Nevada and Idaho. Wagon-wheel ruts are still visible, etched into the lava cap.

A burn dump opened for business in the early 1890s just off of Humboldt. Initially, it was a 10-acre parcel owned by the City of Chico, and operated as the city dump. Household and commercial waste from Chico and the surrounding county was dumped on the site, burned and leveled. Dumping was not limited to the 10-acre site, but also happened on several neighboring, privately owned parcels of land.

The city leased the dump to Butte County until 1964, until the site closed the following year. In 1965, the county opened the Neal Road landfill, which is still in use today.

For most of it's existence, Humboldt Road burn dump was far away from any habitation. However, Chico has continued to grow. The once-remote burn dump is now surrounded by residential neighborhoods., and hundreds of nearby acres are slated for development. How Chico deals with this historic but potentially hazardous site and any future development is a matter of ongoing discussion among concerned citizens.

The first street paved in Chico was on the corner of 2nd and Main Streets.   27

The City of

Chico used to be called the City of Roses. Somewhere along the way, townspeople began to refer to Chico as the City of Trees. It is not known exactly when Chico metamorphosed from the City of Roses to the City of Trees. Local historian, John Nopel, has estimated the name change happened somewhere during the 1930s.

Marcia Wilhite

Marcia Wilhite

Yellow

In the western United States, the yellow rose spoke of love familiar, humble, native to the land. The yellow rose is the prairie rose, the remote rose, it is the extraordinary in the ordinary. It bears a beauty equal to that of other roses, but also speaks of home, of the too-often-overlooked glories of domestic happiness.

What about the roses? Chico became a show place of agriculture and horticulture during the late 1800s. Naturally, any gardener can tell you that roses love a lot of sun and warm weather. The plants can't get enough of it. And that's what Chico offers these gorgeous flowers, lots of sun and of course, the inevitable heat.

Red

When the poet Robert Burns compared his lover to a red, red rose, he was touching on the West's most ancient and potent flower lore, the identification of the red rose with beauty and with deep and passionate love.

From ancient days, long before words complicated what we say to each other, roses have been our messengers, invested with our most cherished feelings. The long, hot days in Chico, has for many years contributed to the abundance of floral delight throughout our local gardens. Annie Bidwell hovered throughout her rose garden during the early 1900s. Rosedale Elementary School was built in 1953 in what was called the "rose district" of Chico. Many Chico homes throughout the years have had outstanding displays, such as that of current local resident, Dr. James Wood, who tends to over 200 rose bushes in his backyard. (The author used to baby-sit his three children.) And of course, there is the tremendous rose garden on the Chico State campus.

White

The white rose suggests purity and silence. White has always expressed qualities of beyond the physical-love beyond the body, love of the soul. The white rose is sometimes called "the flower of light."

Marcia Wilhite

Ty Barbour, ER

Chico is 2 miles from the foothills of the Sierra Nevada.   29

Ty Barbour

Ty Barbour

"I *think that I* shall never see a poem as *lovely as a tree* **"**
—Joyce Kilmer

30

Chico ER

Nopel Collection

The City of *Trees*

If you look back to old, old Chico, there were few trees in the early photographs. Indeed, the surrounding land was adorned with oak trees and orchards, but the area in which houses were built was relatively stark. It was John and Annie Bidwell that wanted trees to line the city streets. This is a tradition that continues to this day. Chico has avenues of big, beautiful trees, in every direction, all over town. John Bidwell continually experimented with planting trees and shrubs and it was he who planted many of the trees along the Esplanade. Today, we can attribute the abundance of trees to John Bidwell and to the subsequent like-minded homeowners who have tended to and planted trees on their property. The city streets are now lined with well-established trees.

Oak Trees

In its natural state most of the acreage in Chico was originally adorned with oak trees. Many seedlings spread across the land that later became known as upper Bidwell Park. The Mechoopda Indians tended to groves of oaks on this land. They roasted acorns of the trees generous yield. The Mechoopda were known to spend sacred hours beneath the shaded limbs in prayer. Though much of the land has been developed due to the expansion of Chico, it still bares a spiritual quality.

Marcia Wilhite

Bidwell Park has a total of 3,670 acres, the third largest municipal park in the United States

Large
Trees

Nopel Collection

Hooker Oak Tree

The legendary Hooker Oak was named after renowned English botanist, Sir Joseph Hooker. A friend and colleague of John Bidwell, Hooker visited Chico in 1877, riding horseback alongside of John Bidwell to view the great oak that resided on Bidwell's land. It was then that Hooker proclaimed the magnificent tree the largest California White Oak (Quercus lobata) in the world. Shortly after, Dr. C.C. Parry, an American Dendrologist, proudly referred to the oak as the Sir Joseph Hooker Oak.

Due to the massiveness of its structure, the tree collapsed on May 1, 1977. Ironically, after the fallen oak was examined, it was discovered that it was not really one tree, but two trees growing together. Today, in remembrance of the Hooker Oak, stands a monument along side a children's playground.

Hooker Oak Elementary School was built in 1948 and named in honor of the oak. Businesses, clubs, and children's sports teams were named either while the massive oak was standing, or in tribute of the big tree. The Hooker Oak Tree is a part of Chico's history that will never be forgotten.

Ty Barbour, ER

Gigantic Walnut Tree

This 80-foot-tall, octogenarian walnut tree sits on a six-acre vacant lot on the north side of Eighth Street between Forest Avenue and the Chico Creek Nature Center. It is a rare species of the walnut variety called a Bastogne, after the French city.

Ty Barbour, ER

Scott Wineland and his assistant carefully prune the tree.

It is also referred to as a paradox walnut. Although it is not known exactly how long the colossal tree has been alive, it has been estimated that it is at least 80 years old. A local arborist has predicted that this giant should live another 200 years. This remarkable tree not only still bares fruit but yields three different types of nuts, as it is partly a graft and partly a hybrid. Although this area is designated for development, the city of Chico's tree ordinance protects the tree. Developer and longtime Chicoan, J.D. Zink, is taking it to the next step by making the tree a centerpiece of his project, rather than just working around it. His commendable goal is to instill as much as possible of Bidwell Park's aura into the atmosphere of his development.

The median age in Chico is 24.6   33

The U.S. Department of Agriculture Genetic Resource Center

aka The Tree Farm

The Tree Farm property is one of Chico's hidden treasures. Those who currently take advantage of it understand its beauty. For those who have forgotten about it, they are now officially reminded. And for those who have yet to experience a short walk on the trail, they will want to do so. Many of the plants at The Tree Farm were planted by the United States Department of Agriculture Introductory Program, which began in 1904. Plants from around the world were brought to Chico, planted, and carefully observed over many years to test their ability to adapt to the environmental conditions of this area. Trees and plants that are propagated on the site today are added to the trail to maintain the beauty and ensure that future generations will be able to learn from and take pleasure in the Nature Trail. There are picnic tables and benches located along the trail for visitors to sit, rest, enjoy the sounds, and spectacular scenery.

The tree farm is a quiet refuge located off the Skyway in Chico.

Marcia Wilhite

Migratory birds can be seen in their nests perched high above the ground as bare branches are exposed during the winter. There is an abundance of wildlife that includes birds, snakes, rabbits, squirrels, rodents, insects and many other species. California Wild Grape vines adorn many areas along the trail and the wide variety of other vegetation enhances the wildlife habitat.

Marcia Wilhite

Marcia Wilhite

Colorful Pistachio Trees along the *Midway*

Marcia Wilhite

Marcia Wilhite

On February 13, 1922 upon the request of the Chamber of Commerce as part of a county road beautification project, two hundred men planted two hundred trees, most of which are still thriving today. For years, these two rows of pistachio trees standing on both sides of the Midway have been a source of admiration, especially in the autumn when the foliage assumes vivid colors of gold and scarlet.

The first house in the city of Chico was built in 1867 and located near the corner of Main and 5th Streets.   35

Ty Barbour, ER

Ty Barbour, ER

Chico

Weather...

Simply Gorgeous

4.

Seasons

Each season brings a unique picturesque landscape to appreciate.

Winter is usually mild, but can get frosty and even snows on rare occasion.

In the spring, colorful flowers are in bloom.

The cooling waters ease the summer heat.

The fall leaf colors rival those in New England.

Many Chicoans look forward to the ever-changing holiday and seasonal displays at this home near the entrance to Bidwell Park.

Chico is *Hot*

Chico is a beautiful place to live. It is sunny and clear over 220 days a year. Like other central valley California towns, however, the sun really comes out in its full glory in July and August. An air conditioner becomes your best friend and there is never a better time for skinny-dipping in Bear Hole (Sorry, no pictures). Chico is HOT!

Nopel Collection

Circa 1915

Ty Barbour, ER

In the early 1900s, before the streets were paved in downtown Chico, a water wagon was used to spray the dust down. A fun summer day activity for the young children of Chico was to play in the sprinkling water that came from the tank on the wagon, cooling down from the extreme Chico heat. Renowned local historian, John Nopel, was one of these children.

On July 23, 1931 the thermometer climbed to a grueling 111 degrees. (Not entirely uncommon for a July day in Chico.) It was this same day in July when a Mrs. A.R. Waters, wife of Dr Waters, then mayor of Chico, decided to prepare her husband's favorite dessert. She dreaded heating up the house by using her wood cooking stove, but knowing of her husband's fondness for caramel custard, she came up with a creative way to satisfy his sweet tooth and keep her home from getting even hotter. After she had mixed up the caramel custard ingredients, she placed the custard in a glass bowl and then positioned the dish outside her home on the cement sidewalk at twelve noon. At exactly one o'clock, Mrs. Waters had one of the most delectable, deliciously baked custards imaginable!

Between its intense summer and mild winter, Chico is generally blessed by colorful and vibrant spring and autumn seasons. Though winter snowfall is not frequent, its occasional happenstance invariably excites the local populace.

Average annual rainfall in Chico is 25.75 inches.

Ty Barbour, ER

Sometimes it's *Not*

Chico has an average of 219 clear days in a typical year.

Teichert

Pond

Ty Barbour, ER

Ty Barbour, ER

Ty Barbour, ER

This unusual marshland and pond is located west on Highway 99 with the Chico Mall on the south and Little Chico Creek on the north. If driving on Highway 99 north and you take a glance to the right below the freeway, the pond is somewhat of a surprise as it lays smack dab in the middle of so much development. Home to many ducks, fish, swallows, blackbirds, frogs, turtles, and even a few beavers, the water is also inhabited with ravenous mosquitoes. In the springtime there is an unusual population of flowering plants that bloom in shades of purple, yellow, and lavender, on tall stalks reminiscent of thistle.

This little wildlife oasis was ironically a result of development, created by huge trucks that were hauling off gravel for the nearby freeway. Their work created a huge cavity that eventually became a wetland area that persisted and was named for Teichert Ready Mix. The marsh area, which at one time used to dry up during the summer months, now remains saturated because of storm water drainage from nearby development. The lake itself is only about four feet deep in most areas, although at one point it reaches a depth of about 40 feet.

Owner of the land, local developer Harry Kassebaum, would like to give the city of Chico the 23-acre parcel that includes not only Teichert Pond, but also the surrounding marshland for an urban wildlife refuge. The primary intent is to preserve a unique wildlife habitat. Kassebaum's gift comes with his request that the city exchange future park credits on some of his other developments. It is Kassebaum who gave the city the land for 20th Street Park, as well as the linear park along the north bank of Little Chico Creek.

Chico is 2 miles from the foothills of the Sierra Nevada.   41

The **Big Fish**

Ty Barbour

Ty Barbour

The big secret ... there's a barn owl that has taken up residence inside of the fish.

We've all seen it and used it as a landmark. "The Big Fish." Located on Highway 32 heading east out of Chico, this enormous catfish has been there almost 20 years. It's one of those things that may not be around forever. But it has sure been fun to say, "There's the fish," to our children.

Why is it there? Originally there was going to be a catfish farm in the orchard where the big fish sits. The land was sold and there is now a private water ski lake hidden away behind the trees.

Wild Game

In the early 1900s, California did not have any laws concerning hunting. People believed that there was a never-ending supply of game and that it would go on forever. Wild game was served in the finest restaurants all over the country.

Ty Barbour, ER

Waterfowl

Farmlands, particularly rice fields, are critical to the survival of migratory waterfowl in California. Millions of ducks, geese, swans, and other species make the Chico area their hometown during the winter. The farmers in Butte County are extremely generous  with the wintering birds. After harvest, many flood their fields to provide waterfowls in the area with a bountiful food supply. Different rice fields are flooded at varying depths to provide a variety in habitat. In Butte County, there is more than 86,000 acres of rice land. After harvest, over 300 pounds per acre usually remains in the field. That, combined with 250 pounds of natural food per acre, supplies the birds with ample nutrients during the cold winter months.

Ty Barbour, ER

Ty Barbour, ER

Ty Barbour, ER

Wildlife

Humans are fascinated by the great diversity of wildlife around them. We are fortunate to be able to experience this pleasure in Chico and its surroundings. The deer that meander through the park. The rich habitat of the Sacramento River. There is no yardstick to measure the aesthetic, cultural, and spiritual values of human contact with other living creatures. These intangible values are personal, touching us in individual ways. Wildlife has a permanent place in our culture. It is our responsibility to respect the importance of our wildlife resources to ensure that future generations are able to enjoy it.

Ty Barbour, ER

Downtown Chico is 8 miles from the Sacramento River.   43

The Sacramento River

During the gold rush a vast amount of mining for gold and other minerals took place along the Sacramento River. Also referred to as the Western Mississippi, the Sacramento River is regarded as a prized element of Chico's history. Just eight miles from the city of Chico, the river was used for transportation and as a source of trade for initial settlers.

Ty Barbour

Ty Barbour

Ty Barbour

Once hunted near the point of extinction, beavers have made an extraordinary comeback. Many have made their home in the Sacramento River. They are resilient and hardworking animals, building impressive lodges, some almost four feet in length. Their industrious nature is not loved by all, however, as their handiwork can damage refuge water control structures and affect the habitat used by other wildlife.

Nature lovers can readily enjoy the pleasures of the Sacramento River. Water activities are plentiful, the scenery is beautiful and the wildlife is abundant. If you stand quietly near the water, you're bound to see a fish jump, or a beaver swim by. Even otters have found a home along the river. For bird watchers, there are great blue herons, egrets, hawks, ducks, and swallows.

John Scott, a Chico native who owns Scotty's Boat Landing, stands at "the Washout," a generous strip of peaceful land where one can simply walk or picnic on the quiet rocky beach right next to the serene flow of the Sacramento River. Wildlife is abundant, and the sound of singing birds creates a backdrop of nature's own music. Many fishermen have frequented this spot for years. Unfortunately, this scenic location becomes a dumping ground for tubers each year after they float down the river on Labor Day. It is the popular place to emerge from the river with an inner tube in tow and too many simply and unthoughtfully just leave their tubes at the Washout.

"Where HAPPINESS and *contentment* seemed to rein in *wild* romantic splendor"

—Osborne Russell, 1835 in Journal of A Trapper

In 1984, the Guinness Book of World Records recorded Chico to have the most (60,000) tubers. 45

Annie's

Bidwell Park Dedication

The third largest municipal park in the United States, Bidwell Park originally occupied 2500 acres of land. John and Annie Bidwell referred to it as Vallombrosa, after a lovely wooded park in Italy. Chico's Vallombrosa was an area they enjoyed together as a couple throughout their marriage, sharing picnic lunches and riding horseback exploring the region. Annie led nature hikes, teaching the children of Chico the names of wildflowers and trees that adorned the area. They sought to preserve and maintain the beauty of its natural state.

It was Annie Bidwell's fear that with the inevitable growth of Chico someday Chico Creek would be ruined by an excessive demand on the dividend of its waters and the surrounding majestic trees would be harvested and eliminated. It was the Bidwells' love and appreciation of the area that prompted the widow Annie to donate land to the City of Chico with provisions included that would insure its preservation. The largest and most publicized of Annie Bidwell's transactions was, of course, the gift of land adjacent to both sides of Chico Creek from what was then the Cemetery Road to the far eastern boundary at Big Chico Creek Canyon.

The first portion, what we now know as Lower Park was deeded in 1905. The remaining more easterly portion was released in 1908. The families of Chico greeted the announcement of the gift of the parklands with great enthusiasm.

Ty Barbour, ER

A large ceremony for the acceptance gift was on a warm evening in July 1905. Suffragist and activist, Susan B. Anthony, a friend of Annie's and a guest at the mansion, was in attendance. This was Mrs. Anthony's first and only visit to Chico.

Since the time of Annie's gift, the City of Chico has purchased additional land bringing its current size to 3,681 acres. The park follows Chico Creek nearly 11 miles through town and into the foothills.

Courtesy Bidwell Mansion

Ty Barbour, ER

One- and Five-Mile Dams

John Bidwell used sand-filled bags to build the first dams that we now know as One and Five Mile. Both areas were used for swimming during the late 1800s. During the summer of 1918, improvements were started on the existing dam on Chico Creek to create a designated swimming area. The pool was not finished until 1921. In 1919 the road was extended from Second and Fourth Streets to another unimproved swimming area now known as Five-Mile.

Chico ER

The three largest city parks in America are Central Park in New York City, Golden Gate Park in San Francisco, and Bidwell Park in Chico, California. 47

Ty Barbour, ER

Ty Barbour, ER

100

Annie's precious gift—Lower Park celebrates its first 100 years—1905–2005

Years

Ty Barbour, ER

Chico ER

Ty Barbour, ER

Water Skiing at One-Mile?

In September of 1949, the very First Annual Water Carnival took place in Bidwell Park, at Sycamore Pool (One-Mile). The event was a huge success with many Chicoans participating and even more viewing the action. There were exhibitions of water skiing, trick ski riding, and water jumps. In 1955 the festival moved to Horseshoe Lake in Upper Park, as the event had grown in size and the lake was more accommodating.

Thank You
Annie
for **100**
Years

THE GRANT:

"IT IS THE WISH OF THE PARTY OF THE FIRST PART, AND IT IS TO BE FULLY CONSIDERED AND UNDERSTOOD, THAT THE SAID PARK IS THE JOINT GIFT OF HER LATE HUSBAND, JOHN BIDWELL, AND HERSELF TO THE CITY OF CHICO AS A TOKEN OF THEIR LOVE AND AFFECTION, AND THAT THE GRAND WORK OF GOD MAY BE PRESERVED TO HIS GLORY AND THE HAPPINESS AND PLEASURE OF THE PEOPLE OF THE SAID CITY FOR ALL TIME."

Thank you Annie!

Horseback riding in the park is one of the simple joys of life in Chico. The trails in Bidwell Park are versatile, providing equestrians with abundant riding opportunities. The Horse Arena, located near the entrance of Upper Park, has a parking lot for trailers, and a fun training arena.

Marcia Wilhite

Ty Barbour, ER

Ty Barbour, ER

These hungry goats are employed to keep the rapid growth of vegetation in lower park under control.

Ty Barbour, ER

When the cooler fall temperatures bring autumn leaves, beautiful Bidwell Park is especially gorgeous

Ty Barbour, ER

How did Highway 99 end up crossing through the park? Late in 1959 the State of California put a great deal of pressure on the Chico Planning Commission to approve a freeway passage through Lower Bidwell Park. The Commission disagreed and fought hard for the citizens of Chico that lived on a quiet street that was literally to be removed to make way for construction. In March of 1960, Chico commission members were served court summons over their refusal to consider the freeway proposed near Sheridan Avenue. Not only did the state want to remove homes, but also the proposed freeway was to pass directly through beautiful Bidwell Park, obviously interfering with the land's natural state. The state offered to pay for realignment of both North and South Park Drives to accommodate the Highway. The Commission was pressured into signing in agreement. Houses were removed and the neighborhood street became a highway.

Ty Barbour, ER

Oh *Deer*

These long legged animals were named "Mule Deer" because of their large mule-like ears. The deer move into Bidwell Park as cold weather develops, making Chico their hometown during the fall, winter, and spring. They retreat into the hills when the summer temperatures begin to climb. If you take a morning stroll in Bidwell Park's One Mile area, you might just happen upon one of these elegant animals. Considering the flurry of activity that takes place in their domain each day, the deer are relatively calm, often standing silently and watching the runners and even dog walkers pass by.

The first radio station in Chico was KHSL. The station hit the air in 1935.   51

Caper *Acres*

Anyone over 13 years of age must be accompanied by a child.

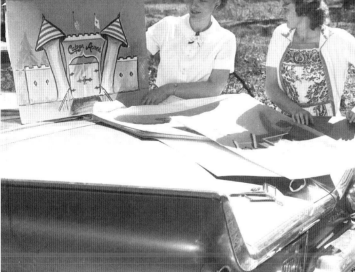

Chico ER

Circa 1958

Caper Acres

It was the Junior Art Club that proposed a children's playground near One-Mile. In April of 1958, members of the club volunteered to paint a fairyland-type theme on the play equipment at a new playground to be called Caper Acres. The original site considered was between the 2nd Street entrance and the proposed Pine Street Bridge. After numerous park committee meetings, the site east of Sycamore Pool at One-Mile was chosen. Today, Chicoans can reflect on almost 50 years of fond memories of either playing at Caper Acres as a child, or sharing the magic with a loved one. Years of birthday parties, Easter egg hunts, 4th of July activities, and picnics with mom and dad at Caper Acres are a part of most every Chicoan's history.

Marcia Wilhite

Children's Park

Annie Bidwell enjoyed the music of children's laughter. Many local children were invited to play in and around the mansion while Annie was alive. It was her love of children that prompted her to establish a playground for the young people in Chico. Just footsteps across the wooden bridge that crosses the creek from the mansion, Annie was known to stroll over to the park to watch the children play. Located in close proximity to the mansion grounds, next to the Presbyterian Church, the Children's Park is still part of the historic landscape. Although the play structures of the park have been updated, the sounds of the nearby creek mixed with the laughter of young children running amongst the tall trees remains much as it did during the days of Annie Bidwell.

"The little ones
leaped and shouted, and laugh'd
And all the hills echoed ... **"**
—William Blake

Ty Barbour, ER

Some Annual Park Events—Mozart Mile,
Bidwell Classic, Almond Bowl Run, 4th of
July Celebration, January 1st Polar Bear
Swim,

Ty Barbour, ER

Upper Park

Upper Park, is located in the majestic canyon where Big Chico Creek flows. Its breath taking views of the valley below, a diverse selection of flora, fauna, and rock formations have made the area a favorite among Chicoans and visitors alike.

Monkey Face

It is in agreement among many of the Chico Park and Recreation Rangers and Directors, that Monkey Face got its name sometime during the 1980s. It is then that kids noticed a similarity to a monkey face on the side of a hill as they were hiking on the North Rim Trail above Horseshoe Lake. Only visible when the surrounding oak trees have lost their leaves, "Monkey Face" can be seen during the late fall and winter. The rock formation is a popular climbing spot with an awesome view of the surrounding area as your reward upon reaching the top. Can you see the chimp?

Ty Barbour, ER

Ty Barbour, ER

Bidwell Park has a different painting for us each day—all pictures of infinite beauty. How fortunate we are to be able to experience a masterpiece of art each time we visit. (And it's free!)

54

Annie's Rules

Known for her strict Christian values, Annie's gift of the park came with a few restrictions. She was specific about the widely known fact that intoxicating liquors were not to be made, sold, or given away in the park. There was to be no hunting. The park was meant primarily for the residents of Chico, but portions could be rented out for cattle ranching. Lastly, there were to be no organized picnics in the park on Sundays.

Ty Barbour, ER

The Golf Course at Bidwell Park

In May of 1920, Chicoan's petitioned the city Park Commission for permission to establish a nine-hole golf course in Bidwell Park. The location suggested was on the north side of Chico Creek, extending to the east from the Five-Mile swimming area. The commission agreed to the proposal and construction began in December of 1920. Private donations and membership fees financed the project. Upon the golf course's grand opening in February of 1921, it became an immediate success. A clubhouse was built in 1925. The Bidwell Park and Playground Commission voted to turn exclusive control of the golf course over to the Chico Golf Association in 1939. In 1948 permission was granted for the course to expand across the road adding another 9 holes. Wildlife abounds in Bidwell Park, and it is not uncommon to see a mother deer and her fawn strolling across the course. Surrounded by rolling foothills amidst the beauty of Bidwell Park's old oak trees, the fabulous scenery of the course is certainly a wonderful bonus to the golf experience.

1949 Hole in One Tournament.

Horseshoe Lake

Horseshoe Lake is located in Upper Park. The site is a terrific spot to start a hike or sit by the water and relax. During the spring, wildflowers bloom in abundance making this area a favorite among locals.

Chico is Dog friendly—

Chicoans are especially crazy about dogs. Yours, his, hers, theirs, or ours, Chicoans love dogs! Drive-thru coffee shops will hand you a bone for your dog as you purchase coffee, sidewalk cafes leave out a bowl of water just for Fido, and a few merchants even keep a stash of doggy treats by the cash register as dogs are welcome to join their owner when they come in to shop. Some folks bring their pooch to work, some to coffee, and some dogs sit outside restaurants patiently awaiting the return of their owner with the

Marcia Wilhite

inevitable "doggie-bag" in hand. The annual Downtown Pet Parade, where dogs are perennially the number one pet registered, is always fun to enter or simply enjoy as a spectator. There is even a monthly walk "for pugs only" in Bidwell Park. The park is a wonderful spot to exercise any size or shape of canine breed. Dog socialization in the park is so strong that, although their paths may cross on a regular basis, it's not uncommon for an owner to know only the name of other dogs, and never be aware of the name of their human companions.

We love cats too—

Since it first began its work in February 1996, The Chico Cat Coalition had as of January 2005, successfully saved 670 cats from Bidwell Park and adopted out 522. Impressive numbers, indeed! The mission of the coalition is to rescue the feral and abandoned domestic cats from lower Bidwell Park, thereby both saving the cat and helping to preserve the natural wildlife of the park. In conjunction with their mission, they provide the rescued cats with veterinary care and spay or neuter the animals, then foster them in loving homes until they are adopted permanently.

The Butte County Humane Society is one of the oldest non-profit agencies in Butte County, working since 1911 to bring humanitarian care to dogs and cats.

Coutesy of Heidi Genasci

Marcia Wilhite

The northside of Upper Park Road is an extraordinary playground for Chico Canines who enjoy running unrestrained. Well-mannered canines and their people can play and hike leash-free.

North Rim Trail

No matter what time of year it is, the North Rim Trail is always an incredible hike. The trail climbs the rugged north rim of Upper Bidwell Park, supplying spectacular views of the canyon and the valley. Mountain bikers can enjoy a series of intense switchbacks, many connecting to Upper Park Road. Equestrians find the scenic terrain a fabulous spot to ride. Most of all, the North Rim is a favorite among dogs and their owners, as this is an area where dogs are allowed "off leash."

Dogs that experience the North Rim Trail give this spot a four paw rating.
🐾 🐾 🐾 🐾

Marcia Wilhite

Ty Barbour, ER

The Easter Cross

Located in Upper Park, near the beginning of the North Rim Trail, the Easter Cross is a mystery to many people. No one seems to know why it is there, or who built it. It is has been documented that the cross has been at its present site approximately 50 years. Originally made from wood, sometime during the 1950s, vandals cut down a cross in the same location. In 1958 it was replaced by a concerned group of citizens who were saddened by its absence. In 1968, the cross was again replaced, this time being made from a surplus light standard that still stands today.

A beautiful rainbow is an appropriate backdrop for the mysterious Easter Cross at the beginning of North Rim Trail.

Ty Barbour, ER

Gorgeous

Grazing

The sowing of seed crops and the planting of trees and vines naturally followed the practice of operating large cattle ranches on the land grants of early Butte County. Livestock farming was predominant in Chico dating back to the late 1840s through the 1850s. John Bidwell owned over 1000 acres of land where he raised cattle. Today, mostly outside of Chico, primarily in the more rural parts of Butte County, livestock raising continues to be an important part of the agricultural process.

Ty Barbour, ER

Ty Barbour, ER

Ty Barbour, ER

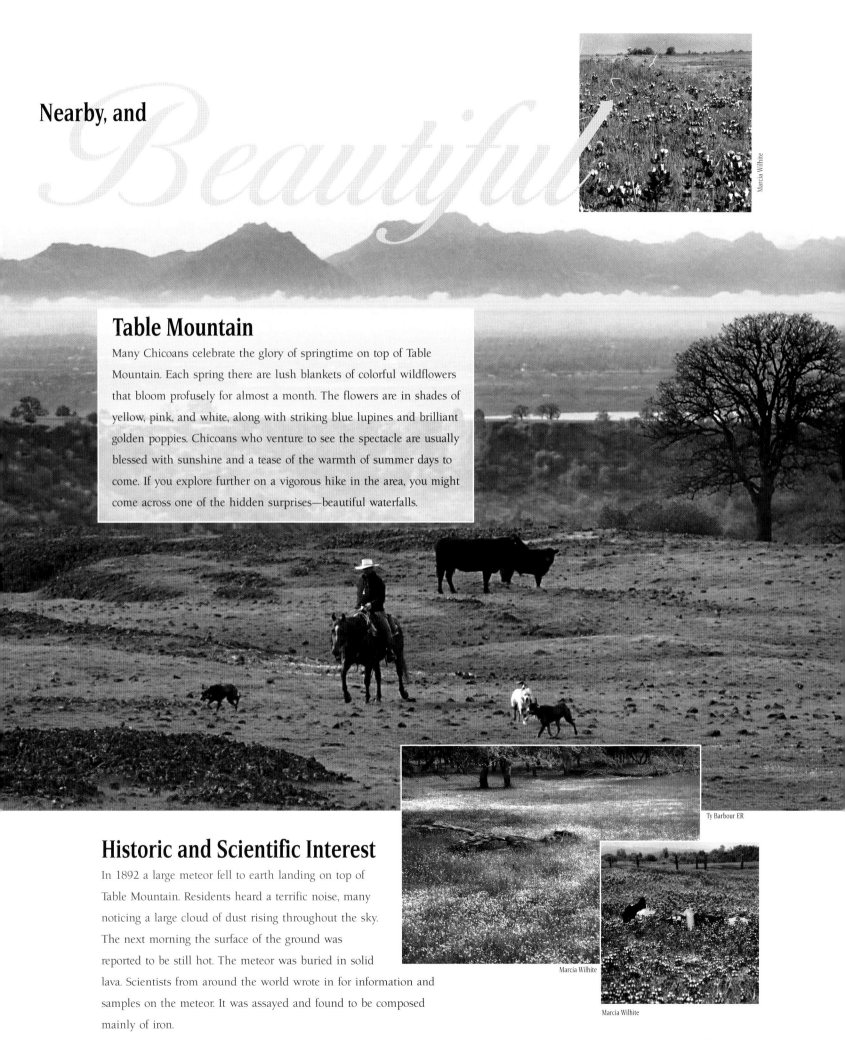

Nearby, and *Beautiful*

Marcia Wilhite

Table Mountain

Many Chicoans celebrate the glory of springtime on top of Table Mountain. Each spring there are lush blankets of colorful wildflowers that bloom profusely for almost a month. The flowers are in shades of yellow, pink, and white, along with striking blue lupines and brilliant golden poppies. Chicoans who venture to see the spectacle are usually blessed with sunshine and a tease of the warmth of summer days to come. If you explore further on a vigorous hike in the area, you might come across one of the hidden surprises—beautiful waterfalls.

Ty Barbour ER

Historic and Scientific Interest

In 1892 a large meteor fell to earth landing on top of Table Mountain. Residents heard a terrific noise, many noticing a large cloud of dust rising throughout the sky. The next morning the surface of the ground was reported to be still hot. The meteor was buried in solid lava. Scientists from around the world wrote in for information and samples on the meteor. It was assayed and found to be composed mainly of iron.

Marcia Wilhite

Marcia Wilhite

By 1967 Mangrove Avenue had become one of Chico's major thoroughfares. 59

The *Wildflower*

Century Bike Ride

An estimated 35,000 cyclists are known to participate in the annual Wildflower Century Ride that takes place in April. It is noted as one of the best rides in the state. Bicyclists from all over the country flood the streets of Chico and the surrounding areas, borrowing large portions of the road for the day. The splendor of the rich spring colors highlighted by the blooming wildflowers in the foothills, along with a challenging ride are the main attraction. The course runs 100 miles, including a loop in Chico, Paradise, and Oroville, then over Table Mountain and back to Chico. This annual event is not just for hard-core cyclists. There are four courses, including a Child Flower, which is a 20-mile ride geared towards families.

Wildflower Bike Ride photos, Ty Barbour, ER

Marcia Wilhite

Located south of East Park Avenue and Park Avenue, local artists Mabrie Ormes and Scott Teeple have created a colorful mural along one of the Wildflower ride paths. Ormes and Teeple worked together to design the mural that pays tribute to an event that has taken place in Chico since 1981. The 200-foot-long wall has been divided in half by the artists work. Teeple's side consists of an aerial view of the landscape of Butte County where the Wildflower Century course runs. Ormes's side is a close-up view of the six habitats of Butte County that are well known for their spectacular show of wildflowers. The mural project was a partnership between the Wildflower Century organizers, Chico Velo Cycling Club, and the City of Chico.

What is it about Chico and the YoYo?

Chico is the epicenter for American Yo-Yoing.

Ty Barbour

Fun Facts:

The world's largest wooden Yo-Yo resides in Chico. This awesome Yo-Yo weighs 256 pounds. It is located at the National Yo-Yo Museum, inside "Bird in Hand," on Broadway.

America's premier Yo-Yo contest takes place in Chico each year during the fall. Yo-Yo enthusiasts travel from all over the world to participate in this incredible event. Yo-Yo players are truly an international community. Players have been known to refer to themselves as "the largest subculture that nobody seems to know about."

Over 80 years of history and artifacts of the Yo-Yo are on exhibit at the National Yo-Yo Museum in Chico. The Museum features the Duncan Family Collection and the Tom Kuhn Collection.

In 2002 Chicoan, Thad Winzenz, was named "America's Best Yo-Yo Instructor."

The Chico Yo-Yo Club is the oldest and longest running Yo-Yo club in the United States. It was started in 1988 by Chicoan, Bob Malowney. In 2002 the National Yo-Yo League, based in Chico, was formed to standardize various regional, national and world contest championships.

Kite Day

Every year in March, the sky in Chico brightens up with colorful kites floating through the air on Kite Day at the Community Park off East 20th Street. The beauty of the day is that it is an event for everyone. Young and old come out to play. Toddling children make their first attempts at flying a kite as parents glow with pride. It's great fun to bring a picnic lunch and enjoy the first moments of spring while relaxing with friends and family at this unique Chico event.

Kite Day photos, Ty Barbour, ER

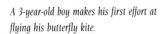

A 3-year-old boy makes his first effort at flying his butterfly kite.

And what about those *Kites!*

Ty Barbour, ER

Ty Barbour

Ty Barbour, ER

Ty Barbour

Durham Almond Industry

Butte County became one of the leading almond-producing counties in the state during the early 1900s. In about 1875 almonds were first planted at Durham, in a small home orchard, by Judge Pratt, the former owner of the famous Aguas Frias Rancho. The first commercial scale of almonds in the Durham district begun in 1895. In 1909, the Durham Almond Growers' Association was formed. Nine years later, this association became affiliated with the California Almond Growers' Association. In 1913, according to the state horticultural commissioner, Butte County produced thirteen percent of the almonds in California.

It's pronounced: **"Amins"**

Almonds

Ty Barbour, ER

The kiwi was introduced in 1967 in Chico.   65

Our *Farms*

This historic water tower is located at the M&T Ranch off of Chico River Road.

Spraque, Chico, Cal.

Circa 1905   Nopel Collection

Ty Barbour, ER

Ty Barbour, ER

Ty Barbour, ER

Ty Barbour, ER

Ty Barbour, ER

Ty Barbour, ER

Ty Barbour, ER

Ty Barbour, ER

Ty Barbour, ER

Ty Barbour, ER

The University Farm

Owned and operated by California State University, Chico, this 1150-acre farm contains an applied research, instructional and production facility to train students and assist the local agriculture industry production.

67

Hmong Farms

The United States transferred the Hmong people to refugee camps after the Vietnam War. Educated and self-sufficient refugees were allowed to immigrate into the United States, where it was anticipated that their families would soon follow. Hmong families began to arrive in Chico during the late 1970s and early 1980s. The Hmong people had seven tribes, with a chief for each. The Lee tribe was considered among the most influential of them all. In Chico, Kou Lee was the leader and liaison for the Hmong. He spoke five languages, including fluent English. A teacher's aide in the public school system, he worked at Rosedale Elementary for many years, and then transferred to Chapman Elementary. He was extremely influential in teaching English to the Hmong in the area.

The Hmong were farmers in their native land. Sunny skies and farming conditions in Chico were similar to their homeland. Lee and a few of his relatives bought a small piece of property on River Road.

Using labor, instead of machinery and chemicals, the Hmong became entrenched in farming. Their noted labor-intensive, hand nurtured farming techniques have become their trademark. Sweet, delicious strawberries became their most popular crop. Today, Hmong farmers hold a large presence at the Chico Farmer's Market. Children and teenagers help their parents and grandparents to display and sell beautiful flowers and produce.

Hmong Farm photos: Marcia Wilhite

The Hmong culture remains vibrant, as they continue to participate in traditional Hmong holidays and events. However, as it has been throughout the history of America, while the elders strive to preserve their cultural identity, much of the new generation is becoming "Americanized," dressing in trendy American styles and listening to popular hip-hop music. The Hmong youth are increasingly flourishing in the Chico school system, succeeding in both educational and athletic activities.

The Hmong have assimilated into Chico. Many have purchased land and bought homes. Numerous have graduated from the public school system and the university. They have become an integral part of the community and are a welcome addition to Chico, contributing positively to the diversity of our wonderful town.

Farmer's Market photos: Ty Barbour, ER

Farmers' *Market*

The Certified Farmer's Market concept is an effort to re-establish the traditional link between farmers and consumers in California. Put simply, Chico's Farmer's Market is "the real thing," a place where genuine local farmers sell their crops directly to the public. The number one reason Chicoans shop at the Farmer's Market is because of the quality. Fresh picked, vine and tree ripened quality continues to attract the community rain or shine. It is a place to relax on a Saturday morning as you stroll through the downtown market, a cup of coffee in one hand, and a bag full of fresh goodies in the other. A place to see familiar faces, or catch up with a friend from the past.

In addition to seasonal produce from Butte County, there's music, handmade gifts, and baked treats to savor. The Farmer's Market produces a strong sense of community identity, bringing people from diverse ethnic and different backgrounds together. This rare meeting of farmers and consumers serves as an educational experience whereby customers learn about their food sources, have access to nutritional information, engage in multi-cultural experience and become more aware of agricultural issues.

**Thursday Night—
April thru September
Saturday Mornings—
Rain or Shine**.

*In 1954 there were 14,717 acres
of almonds in Butte County.* 69

Chico

Loves to love ...

Lovers Lane

"Wanna' go park and watch the lights?"

Most every town has their own spot—a place to park after dark. Drive east of Chico, up Highway 32, and you will come across a flat gravel parking lot- This is Chico's very own "Lover's Lane." A breathtaking view after dark, the hillside site gives a spectacular display of lights every night. Chico is the star attraction, offering the viewer a beautiful location to "park." On a clear day the spot offers a view all the way to the coastal range. Equally as spectacular are the sunrises. Watch as sunlight replaces starlight. The peacefulness of the city below as the sky changes is phenomenal. During thunderstorms it is an exciting place to watch as lightening radiates throughout the valley below.

Ty Barbour, ER

Mother Nature displays her own show of fireworks.

The Historic Patrick Ranch

... Our rich *History* ...

Patrick Ranch Photos, Ty Barbour, ER

Hester Patrick generously left the Patrick Ranch to the Chico Museum Association in 2001. It is the remainder of two large neighboring pioneer ranches, the 618 acre Northgraves place, and the 1200 acre Wright-Patrick place, which merged in 1958 when Hester's husband, Pat Patrick inherited the Northgraves property.

The Patrick Ranch is a precious piece of Chico's heritage. The Chico Museum Association is working diligently to develop the ranch into a place where people can learn more about local agricultural history, as well as what life would have been like for early pioneers in the area. The Northgraves-Compton house, which resides on the property, is in the process of becoming a historic house museum. Furnishing reflects all 105 years of Compton and Patrick era occupancies. Old receipts, ledgers, and other papers are being researched before making any significant changes.

Good ol' *Fun Scenery!*

and Magnificent

Ty Barbour, ER

A dog-gone good time at Butte Creek.

Butte Creek parallels Centerville and Honey Run Roads in Chico. The scenery is magnificent including interesting rock formations, and there are mine tailings along the creek that date back to the 1800s, although these are mostly covered by vegetation. The water quality is crystal clear and there are usually some fun rapids for tubers. This is a fantastic spot to cool off during the long hot days of summer in the north valley.

Chico *High*

Chico ER

Chico High School

The earliest attempts to establish a high school for the Chico School District were made in 1875 and 1893. Two special bond issues were called in 1896 to raise funds for construction of a new high school. The bond issues failed, as they were unsuccessful at achieving the necessary two-thirds majority vote. In the meantime, a privately financed high school class was being conducted at the old Oakdale School. Then, in 1898, a ninth grade program was added to the public schools curriculum, which further generated interest in high school education. Finally, on April 19, 1902, a successful special election was held in the district whereby Chico High School was established. Plans progressed rapidly, and William M. Mackay was selected to serve as the school's first principal.

Nopel Collection

Photos this page circa 1903–1905

Chico ER

Chico High School began its first session on September 2, 1902, with 46 students in attendance. There were three teachers, one of which taught part-time. For its first few years' classes temporarily met on the third floor of the Oakdale School Building. In April 1905 Chico High School moved to its first permanent building, which was constructed of brick in strong Grecian architectural style. (Where the Meriam Library stands today.) Grand old cherry trees surrounded the school on its three and a half acres, which had been purchased out of the famed Bidwell cherry orchard. The school structure commanded a view of the whole length of High Street. (Currently Hazel.) Among its noted features was a library with a folding wall that opened into an assembly hall that could seat 300 people.

In 1903 the schools' second enrollment had grown to 72 students. The first Student Government was formed that same year. By the end of the school year in 1904, six teachers were on staff due to the influx of students that increased the student body to over 100 pupils. The first graduating class at Chico High had six students. Their commencement took place in 1904 at the City Opera House. (Where the El Rey Theatre stands today.) Also in 1904, the school newspaper, The Red and Gold was first published. Clubs and social activities were a vital part of campus life. Among the most popular were the Mandolin Club, Girls' Glee Club, and Orchestra.

A tradition of community awareness and service emerged in 1906 when much of the students' extra-curricular energies were dedicated to sending help to victims of the Great San Francisco Earthquake.

As was the case with many early buildings in Chico, a fire in January 1911 destroyed the first Chico High School. It was reported that the captain of the football team and several other boys rescued the school records and thirteen trophies. Classes met in the Presbyterian Church for the remainder of the school year. A new building was rapidly built and completed in July that same year.

Circa 1904

Chico ER

Circa 1966

Chico ER

Circa 1968

Chico ER

In 1917 a new tradition of service began when many Chico High students left to join the United States military in the fighting in Europe in World War I. During this time most of the school activities became fundraisers and social events dedicated to supporting the war efforts.

In 1918 the first school band was formed, and the orchestra became a jazz band. There were 500 students in attendance, twenty faculty members, and a graduating class of sixty-six.

The first principal at Chico High School, William Mackay, served thirteen years, leaving in 1915. He was the second longest principal to lead the school until Roger Williams (the author's principal) was at the helm for 25 years.

Chico High has been burned down, torn down, and rebuilt twice. 73

Ty Barbour, ER

California State University

Nopel Collection

The land on which California State University, Chico stands was originally an eight acre cherry orchard owned by the city's founding father, John Bidwell. When the selection of the site had not yet been made it was John Bidwell who said, "You may take anything on my farm but my dooryard." Bidwell donated his prize cherry orchard to the people and city of Chico for the construction of the Normal School. Bidwell was sent a letter expressing the gratitude that the people of Chico felt towards him: "Your gift, free of all charge of expense, covered as it is with the choicest of fruits, constitutes an everlasting monument of interest in the cause of education, and entitles you to the gratitude of Northern California." In 1887 the Chico Normal School was established for the education and training of California public school instructors and administrators.

In the evening of August 12, 1927, the entire Normal School was engulfed by roaring flames. Unfortunately, despite a heroic effort by the local fire department, the original classrooms, laboratories, library, museum, equipment and records were lost forever. When the fire finally burned itself out by dawn, nothing remained but vine-covered exterior walls.

Ty Barbour, ER

74

Andrew Hill, a State of California architect, was directed
to plan new facilities for the campus in 1928. The
present administration building, Kendall Hall, was the
keystone of his plan. Along with Laxson Auditorium
and Ayres Hall to the east, and a library, later named
Trinity Hall, to the west these early buildings now
constitute the heart of the campus.

The city of Chico and the university are inextricably
bound to each other. Chico is the only true campus
town in the state of California. A CSUC student can
step out of class and into the natural elements on
campus central to the splendor of the Chico area—
Tree-lined walkways and gardens, crystal clear creeks,
and impressive views of the distant Sierra and Pacific
coastal range. Only footsteps away from the university
is downtown Chico, a treasure trove of eateries, coffee
houses, boutiques, and fun shops, which are, for the

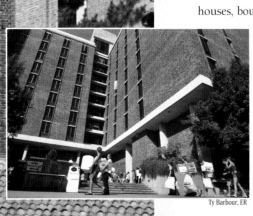

most part, owned by locals. Downtown
would not be nearly as vibrant without
the college. The students can ride their
bikes all over town, and walk to all of
their classes on campus. Chico State
University is a residential
college and the students that live
here immerse themselves into the
Chico community.

In 1938 chimes were installed in the library (Trinity Hall) tower. 75

Pioneer Days

What is now remembered by most Chicoans as Pioneer Days, "Senior Day" was instituted to combat low enrollment at the Normal School in May of 1919. The change in title to Pioneer Days came in 1927. As the university grew, so did Pioneer Week and the size and intensity of the parties associated with the festivities. There was a tendency for the many of the fraternities and sorority members involved to have their lives consumed by the spirited week each year. The influence spread to locals and visitors and the reputation grew that Chico was a good place to party. In 1985, Playboy magazine dubbed Chico State as the #1 Party School in the nation. This is a title that has not been easy to shake. Pioneer Days will remain a fond memory for those who were able to participate and is a loss for those who missed out on the town spirit and college fun.

Though always referred to as a good family community, it is important to remind one that Chico has long had its quota of bars downtown with saloons on every corner and miners celebrating on the streets in the days of the Gold Rush during the 1800s. Chico State has worked hard to overcome its "party school" image. CSUC President Robin Wilson said, "Lets take Pioneer Days out back and shoot it in the head," His successor, President Manuel Esteban, was extremely influential in turning around the reputation of the school. Esteban focused his efforts on an economical education, in the beauty of a small campus, with a community that embraces the college students.

Saloons

As Chico became a hub for early pioneers who came to find their fortune in the Gold Rush, the little town took on the features of a real settlement. During the 1860s, there were many saloons in what we now know as the downtown area. Gambling and other "evils" which follow in their wake also came along to the little town. There was a great deal of drinking that took place. Most of the men drank daily, and it was a common occurrence to see the finest of gentlemen patronize the saloons. There was a great deal of gambling and no laws against it. Draw poker and seven up were the card games of choice. Many women of the "lower sorts" frequented the back rooms of the saloons and freely walked the town without any trouble from the law.

Nopel Collection

Circa 1905

*Normal School
circa 1890.*

Nopel Collection

Ty Barbour

Ty Barbour

In 1972 Chico State College became California State University, Chico as a result of legislation passed in 1971. 77

Corpse Flower

It Stinks! Only in Chico—this fascinating flower has bloomed only once since its arrival in Chico in 1999. When it finally did, it smelled like the dead body that belays its name. California State University, Chico, acquired this rare Indonesian flower when it was a yearling. In eight years of growth at the university, the flower didn't bloom until June 2004. It created quite a flurry of activity as people flocked to the university greenhouse to view (and to smell) the corpse flower that had finally bloomed. The stench was more prominent than the beauty of its three-day bloom activity.

The foul fumes of the Corpse Flower are not constant. They come out in waves as the plant builds up the energy to produce them to attract the insects that will pollinate it. The flower is in the same family as two common plants-the pink calla lily and the arum lily.

Bidwell Bowl Amphitheater

In November 1937, plans were announced for construction of the amphitheater. The federal government provided $3,403 in funds specifically for the project and the Chico Park Commission matched that same amount. City engineer, Frank Robinson, designed the plans for the project. Originally there was a stage, 80 feet by 40 feet, which was located on the north side of the creek. The stage was built in three tiers and positioned on the grass.

Today the amphitheater is owned and managed by the City of Chico. Primarily rented for weddings and small orientations, the amphitheater is also a wonderful spot for university students to sit and study while listening to the peaceful sound of the creek trickle by. Photographer, Ty Barbour and his wife Deb, were married here in 1980.

Ty Barbour, ER

Ty Barbour

Alumni Glen

Ty Barbour

Chico without the university is like a rose without fragrance. The town would be incredibly different without the thriving school and energy that comes from the students of Chico State. Because of the University, Chico is richer, more cultured, more educated, and much more diverse than any similar Central Valley town. It was John Bidwell that had the foresight to bring Normal School to Chico. (Thank you John!) He was progressive and enlightened. He wanted Chico to become a place of higher culture and sophistication.

Chico State not only provides its students with a stimulating environment for an education, it also presents the community and visitors with beautiful architecture and centers for cultural growth. It is the heartbeat of the town. In 1889, the first term began with an enrollment of just 90 students. Today, there are almost 15,000 students. The college has grown into a picturesque campus, offering academic excellence to scholars from fifty states and twenty-five countries.

The late San Francisco Chronicle columnist, Herb Caen, once called Chico "the kind of place where you find Velveeta cheese in the gourmet section at the supermarket." 79

The Depot

The railroad depot in Chico was first built in 1892, after the 1869 depot had been pulled down. It now serves as a small, unattended station for Amtrak. On the walls of the little station are historic photographs of early Chico's railroad.

Chico ER

Chico ER

Nopel Collection

Ty Barbour

Within the same building right next door to the train station is "The Chico Art Center," a combination teaching center and art gallery, sponsored by a community artist group whose main goal is to spotlight art.

Ty Barbour

Chico *Art*

gallery CHICO Art

In 2002, Chico was
named one of the
"Top 100 Best Small
Arts Towns in America."

Ty Barbour

Ty Barbour, ER

Ty Barbour

Artist. Sal Casa strolls into teach an
early morning drawing class..

Twenty Chico State co-ed girls were housed
in Bidwell Mansion during 1932. 81

Marcia Wilhite

Jake Early

Artist Jake Early, has lived in Chico since he was five years old. Early has always been fascinated by the exceptional landmarks that he has seen in Chico. As a young child, he took drawing lessons from a college student who lived on 3rd and Orient Streets.
The landmark he used to find her house was the nearby water towers. At age 30, the same water towers became his first subject he drew and screenprinted when he decided to start a limited-edition print series focusing on his hometown, Chico.

Screenprinting is an ancient practice. Its concept is simple—a cut stencil is placed beneath a fine screen through which paint flows. The stencil's holes allow paint through to print onto paper placed directly below. Today, this age old skill is used in each poster created by Jake Early. After he has completed his drawing, he then photographs his design on film using an old camera, creating stencils and screens from his art. To finish, he prints his product on a press that he built himself, which is fashioned after an antique press design. The completed product is a literal translation of his sketch. A unique trademark marking his creation is to include metallic ink somewhere on each poster. His work is detailed and intricate. From start to finish Early puts his heart and soul into each poster. The result is a gorgeous piece of art that Chicoans have been actively seeking out and purchasing. Not surprisingly, he has sold out of all of his initial pieces.

Marcia Wilhite

Art House 821 Orient Street

Artist, Norm Dillinger has lived in Chico for over 30 years. His home is just a sample of his unique style. It took Norm seven years to paint both the outside and inside of his house.

Marcia Wilhite

Ty Barbour

Public Art

Public art is well woven into the tapestry of Chico. There are magnificent sculptures, glass pieces, and collages created by local artists, which are displayed throughout the town. Many downtown walls have become canvases of beautiful artistic expressions.

In 1864 there were 199 children enrolled in school in Chico. 83

Ty Barbour, ER

Art Show at the annual, Taste of Chico event.

Marcia Wilhite

Main Street Mural by Gregg Payne

Ty Barbour, ER

Lindo Bridge Mural by Gregg Payne

Marcia Wilhite

Ty Barbour

Pastels on the Plaza!

Pastels on the Plaza is an event that is held in September, and organized by the "Parent Education Network." Volunteer artists generously donate their time and talent, lining the sidewalks of the downtown Chico City Plaza. Local businesses sponsor a square on the sidewalk, as a donation to the "Parent Education Network." Entertainment, food, and children's activities enhance the occasion. The event is magical to watch. Many on-lookers are known to spend hours on the plaza, watching in amazement as colorful chalks are used to create beautiful drawings. Each square turns into a unique and magnificent work of art by the end of the day.

Pastel photos, Ty Barbour, ER

Listen to the *Music*

Another Look

" **Music** and **RHYTHM** *find their way* into the secret places of the **SOUL.** "

—Plato

By Christine LaPado

Chico is Northern California's oasis of great music. Geographically isolated from, yet influenced by, the major population and music hubs of San Francisco, Portland, Seattle and beyond, Chico's buzzy scene has everything from folk to rock to jazz to indie to classical music happening on a regular basis—in the bars, cafes and world-class venues like Sierra Nevada Brewery's Big Room, and it's all good, as they say. Names of popular local performers like phenomenal jazz guitarist Charlie Robinson, father and son rockers Greg Scott and Greg Scott II, and rappers The Becky Sagers are as well known around here as brand names.

The rock and alternative scene in this town has long been particularly notable and vibrant. Long-time local musician John LaPado tells the story of when he came to Chico in 1970 as "another carpetbagger, a refugee from the Bay Area."

"I had gotten a slide guitar at the San Jose flea market for 20 bucks," LaPado explains, "and got hooked up through mutual friends with [then-guitarist] Michael Cannon [another Bay Area "refugee"], someone who became a major force in Chico music over the next 30 years." Cannon and LaPado put together a "ragtag hippie band" called the Butte Creek Family Jamboree, playing at places like the now-defunct Odyssey in Chapmantown or the Drop-in Club, now LaSalles. Supa Nova was a band of New Jersey ex-pat rockers playing around town at this same time. Led by lead guitarist Zack Borland, Supa Nova featured drummer Jimmy Fay, bassist Billy Baxmeyer and percussionist Jerry Morano, who would go on to form the legendary band Spark 'n' Cinder with Cannon.

Chico in the '70s was a "counter-culture hotbed," as LaPado tells it. "People loved to go see their friends in the band ... Extended jams and conceptual 'happenings' were prevalent, as well as political posturing against war and 'the Establishment,' and general dance fever and pure abandonment. Who knows how many babies were born [as a result] of shows by Spark 'n' Cinder, Prairie Biscuit, George Souza, Peter Berkow or the Ralph Shine Blues Band?"Fast forward to the '80s as the increasingly complex and at times overly self-indulgent hippie music scene began to give way to punk rock and New Wave music. Punk bands like Vomit Launch and 28th Day (featuring widely known indie queen Barbara Manning), reflecting the trends of the music world at large, hit the scene with their edgy, original sounds. The New Wave of musicians stepped up with their upbeat, ska sound tinged somewhat with the jaded world view of the punk rockers. The Night Knights-Scott Pressman (Ska-T) on guitar, Prairie Biscuit's Kim Gimbal (Kid Crash) on drums and Supa Nova's Baxmeyer (Dik Slax) on bass—were a prime example of the New Wave sound, playing infectious originals along the lines of the UK's The Police and Joe Jackson. At the same time, however, good ol' local staples like Cottonwood, Craig Strode's country-rock group, just kept on doing their thing, playing the county fairs and firemen's balls, while the

Duffy's St. Patrick's Day, 2005.

Nelson and Sugar

Ska-T

Greg Scott II

Holly and Eric

hippies, punk rockers and New Wavers were battling it out in the bars. Ditto for the straight-ahead rock-and-roll of Matt Hogan and the Incredible Diamonds, and blues band The Road Rockets, featuring the husband and wife duo of Nelson & Sugar, who were active on the local blues scene as well as out of town.

Music photos courtesy of Greg Scott, Greg Scott II, Kim Gimbal, Valerie St. George, Holly Taylor, and Moriss Taylor

Chico's music scene continued to grow and become more diverse. The Funnels, the outrageous and funky Brutilicus Maximus, The Butte Creek Sextet (with the soulful Stevie Cook on vocals and guitar), among numerous others, appeared on the scene, each with their own big and devoted following.

The '90s saw a band come straight out of the Chico State dorms to go on to great success.

Grammy-winning Dobro player Sally Van Meter came out of The Colby Mountain String Band. The recently departed Jimmy Borsdorf was a champion fiddler who, along with his wife Nancy, also a fiddler, were known as Hawks and Eagles, and played their own "cowboy gypsy" music. Ex-Night Knight Kim Gimbal currently plays mandolin in popular bluegrass band Mossy Creek.

Long popular on the jazz scene, in addition to guitarist Robinson, has been Charlie Haynes, the "boss man" of the alto sax, flute and clarinet, whose March 2005 move to Austria leaves a not-easily-filled hole. Other jazzers with devoted followings are the wife-husband duo of singer Holly Taylor and guitarist Eric Peter, and alto sax man Rudy Giscombe. Multi-instrumentalist Greg D'Augelli is always in demand when he's not out of town on a gig or doing high-profile session work.

Not to be forgotten is the "Blue Kahuna," the late Danny West, whose idiosyncratic style in both performance and attire, endeared him to countless people. Danny West and the Lonesome Cowboys' unique brand of raunchy 3-chord blues featured West's raspy voice and raucous piano playing, and entertained the crowds "like a mutha," as West might say.

Chico remains a vibrant, eclectic hotbed of music of all kinds. Bands like the popular "emo" band Number One Gun, rockers Thirst, and twisted troubadour Dan Cohen continue to bring the sounds of Chico to the outside world via touring and record contracts. This is the town that spawned both the raging metal band Red With Envy and Duffy's Tavern's Friday afternoon Irish regulars The Pub Scouts, as well as the funky, ska-punky Fat Chick From Wilson Phillips and neo-hippie jam band Electric Circus. And Bone Gruel. And Moriss Taylor. **Gotta love it.**

—Christine LaPado

Greg Scott

The Mother Hips' country-tinged California rock sound landed the band a major label record contract as well as a huge following, both locally and nationwide, which continues to this day, despite the band's breakup.

Bluegrass and old-timey music have woven a consistent thread through Chico's music scene over the years. The 8th Avenue String Band, a perennial favorite, was the early musical "stomping ground" of award-winning yodeling cowboy accordion player Sourdough Slim (a.k.a. Rick Crowder).

Kim Gimbal

Moriss Taylor at 17 and at 7—an ageless Chico icon.

Moriss Taylor

Fifty years ago you could turn on your black and white television set and see Moriss Taylor singing and dancing.

Today, he's still to be found on television screens (though some are flat screen plasmas) and he looks almost exactly the same! Moriss's signature jet black hair is still swooped to the side, he wears a cowboy hat placed properly atop his head, and is always in a snazzy cowboy shirt. His corny jokes have had the folks in Butte County laughing since 1948. Combined with his sunny disposition and country and western style of singing, he is a local celebrity. He has many loyal fans, with some who have followed him since the beginning of his career and a younger generation of groupies who maintain the Moriss Taylor legend. After much convincing by devoted admirers, Moriss has released two CDs, titled "Moriss Taylor's Original New Cowboy Music" and "Moriss Taylor's Fun and Love Songs."

87

Chimes in Chico

The ancient Chinese were excellent metal workers (dating back to as early as 1,000 B.C.) they created something that would eventually become a garden décor item that is today found in 85% of United States households.

In the late 19th century a musician sought to improve the tone of the bells he played in an orchestra. He suspended metal rods of varying lengths from a rack and found that resonance increased.

Chimes at Zucchini and Vine

Entrepreneurial Victorians, remembering the furin of the Chinese, were quick to put two and two together and the modern wind chime was born. It was immensely popular, and today wind chimes are the single most purchased garden décor accessory in the world.

Many Chicoans are fond of the beautiful wind chimes that dangle at the corner of 2nd and Main, in front of Zucchini and Vine. An item that is regularly sold in the store, they are a comforting fixture on the downtown corner. It is often that a parent is seen holding their baby up to the chime as the child sparkles in amazement. If you stop to take a rest at the store's corner bench, (or wait for a loved one to shop) you can enjoy rich, harmonious chimes sweeping into a song from the metal pipes.

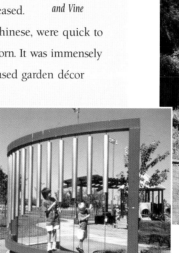

Chimes at Wild Wood Park

Gregg Payne's collosal wind chime

Chimes photos, Marcia Wilhite

The *Movies*

The Pageant Theatre

A favorite among locals, the Pageant Theatre is located on the corner of 6th Street and Flume. It's a quaint little movie house, situated just off downtown, showing just two flicks a night, usually independent or foreign features. Monday night is a bargain! The tickets are only $2.50 a seat. A great combination is to catch a good foreign film at the Pageant, and afterwards stroll down to 7th Street for an ice cream cone at Shubert's.

Pageant Theatre photos, Marcia Wilhite

Adventures of Robin Hood

The film starred Errol Flynn, Olivia de Havilland, Claude Rains, and Basil Rathbone. Bidwell Park doubled as the Sherwood Forest. You can find Robin Hood Glade, located on the north side of Big Chico Creek near where Highway 99 crosses the park. The famous fight scene that took place between Robin Hood and Little John was in all actuality at Big Chico Creek. Perhaps the greatest costume adventure of all time, the film was released in 1938.

The splendid color photography, sets, and costumes are all first-rate, effectively transporting us back to an enchanting world. That world was in little Chico, California. The city of Chico celebrated the filming completion by throwing a big party for Warner Brothers. (True Chico style!) The town renamed the north part of Ivy Street to Warner Street. Chico has treasured the success of the motion picture ever since.

Robin Hood photos courtesy Chico Museum

Marcia Wilhite

Robin Hood in Sherwood Forest mural at West Fourth Street—between Main and Broadway commemorates the 50th Anniversary of the filming of "The Adventures of Robin Hood." (Mural by Scott Teeple 1988)

Gone With The Wind

It was 1939 in Chico, California. The film Robin Hood had been released just one year previous, and had been a phenomenal success. Film directors found Chico as a site to create yet another major motion picture melodrama based on Margaret Mitchell's epic novel, "Gone With The Wind." The sweeping romantic melodrama follows the ever-changing fortunes of southern belle Scarlett O'Hara (Vivian Leigh) who falls in love with the suave and cynical Rhett Butler (Clark Gable) as she struggles to protect her family's plantation from the ravages of the Civil War. Gerald O'Hara's (Thomas Mitchell) first horseback ride was filmed in Bidwell Park. Other picture locations in this area include: Bidwell Park Golf Course, Richardson Springs, Pentz Road, and a Paradise apple orchard.

In July of 1923, $25,000 was granted by the state for the purchase of Bidwell Mansion for the use of Chico State Normal.

El Rey Theatre

This historic building was a posh spot to attend when it first opened in 1905. In those days, it was a sophisticated show house known as the Majestic Theatre. Many of the finest musical and dramatic troupes of the era performed in Chico at the Majestic. The original seating capacity of 800 included both upper and lower windowed box seats. Originally three stories tall, the second floor housed a club and banquet room, with the building's owner, the Elks Club, occupying the third floor. In 1946, a fire blazed through the building, burning it to the ground.

It was rebuilt in 1929 as a two-story structure and renamed the National, and then renamed again as the American in 1939. The motion picture Robin Hood was released in 1939, and people packed the house at the American to see the movie that had been filmed before many of their eyes right here in Chico.

Circa 1939

Circa 1905

Circa 1948

Circa 1949

Historic theatre photos courtesy of Eric Hart

Ty Barbour

When the theatre was reconstructed after the fire in 1947, artists James Seaton and Martin Ravenstein painted the fairy and elf faces on the walls and ceiling. They were asked to create a magical theme of oil paintings inside the theatre. And magical, indeed, were the fairies that seemed to dance on the walls as the lights dimmed to show the current featured film.

In 1948 when the company that owned the building closed their Bay Area theatre called the El Rey, they brought their sign up to Chico to be worn on this 2nd Street location, and gave it the name that was used for the last 57 years. Oddly enough, the bay area theatre had also burned to the ground.

Circa 1949

Change is inevitable. As large corporations have moved into our community many smaller businesses have struggled to stay open. The El Rey's popularity declined over the last few years due in part to competition from newer state-of-the-art, multi screened theatres. This eventually led the Regal Entertainment Group of Knoxville, Tennessee, to put the El Rey up for sale.

During the design process of this book, Eric Hart and Tom Van Overbeek purchased the El Rey building. Hart was raised in Chico, and has experience dealing with historic buildings, having renovated the Ballroom on Broadway, in the old Odd Fellows Hall. He also owns the Senator Theatre, which is still in the process of its renovation. Big plans are in store for the El Rey. With the new owners alongside, local architect/engineer, David Griffith and Associates hopes to transform the building into a "modern historic" structure with significant overtones of the original Majestic. The old name is being revived and it will be called the Majestic Building. Current plans illustrate underground parking, retail and professional office space.

Many long-time Chicoans carry fond memories of the El Rey from its hey-day. The 1975 summer hit movie "Jaws" had people lined up around the entire city block. Star Wars seemed to be on the marquis for at least a year. And then, of course, there was the ever popular, "Rocky Horror Picture Show" that played at mid-night for years.

Chico said goodbye to the El Rey on March 3, 2005. The last movie shown was the award winning comedy, "Sideways." The seats were filled with Chicoans (author included) who were taking pictures with their cell phones and digital cameras. Much of the talk was about the "good old days," first dates, "making out" in the balcony, and naturally, the beautiful murals on the walls. The future may appear grim for the fairies and elves, but hopefully they will never be forgotten, as their faces will shine on in the memory of many local theater patrons.

The first marriage license issued in Butte County was in 1862. 91

"THE FUTURE belongs *to those who believe in the* beauty OF their *Dreams!*"

—Eleanor Roosevelt

As Governor of California, Ronald Reagan visited Chico in 1967.

Ronald Reagan

In 1966 Ronald Reagan was elected Governor of California by a margin of a million votes; he was re-elected in 1970. In 1980 he won the Republican Presidential nomination. A renewal of national self-confidence by 1984 helped Reagan and Bush win a second term in the nation's highest office with an unprecedented number of electoral votes.

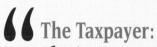

The Taxpayer:
That's someone who works for the federal government but doesn't have to take the civil service examination.

—Ronald Reagan

John F. Kennedy

The handsome young senator from Massachusetts had his work cut out for him during his trip across the country as he campaigned as the Democratic Candidate for the 1960 Presidential Race. Along the way he made a brief stop in Chico to speak.

**Ask not what your country can do for you—ask what you can do for your country.**

—John F. Kennedy

In 1939 Mrs. Roosevelt rode in on the train to meet with Chicoans.

Eleanor Roosevelt

"What other single human being has touched and transformed the existence of so many? She walked in the slums and ghettos of the world, not on a tour of inspection, but as one who could not feel contentment when others were hungry."   —Adlai Stevenson

An important *Whistle Stop*

Arnold Schwarzenegger, Governor of California, visited Chico in 2004.

Chico received national attention when GOP candidate Bob Dole fell from the stage onto a group of supporters. Apparently, the candidate's security had removed the nails from a hand railing that was built to stand between Dole and the crowd. The idea was that if an overzealous supporter tried to jump up on stage the person would fall from lack of stability of the railing. A reverse action took place. No one explained this tactic to Bob Dole. The unknowing Dole leaned against the railing and fell into the crowd. It shocked everyone, especially Mr. Dole! Supporters caught him and though momentarily stunned, he quickly regained his composure and was able to give his speech.

In 1935, Chico State held classes inside Bidwell Mansion.   93

Whenever towns were established, it was always the most responsible citizens that were chosen to work for the fire department. In the late 1800s only men filled the positions of firefighters. The firemen of centuries past had no easy task. In those days, there were no building codes or hazard awareness programs. Water supplies were distant and meager. The use of coal and wood as fuel exposed every home to daily danger.

In March of 1873, the Chico Board of Trustees called a meeting for the purpose of organizing a fire company. The 44 individuals who attended were among Chico's most prominent businessmen, clerks, and mechanics. That same month, just weeks before the town's largest fire, Company No. 1 was formed.

The midnight sky on April 19, 1873, was brilliant with flame. The fire began in the hayloft of the Fashion Stable at Third and Main, burning so rapidly that the stable hands barely escaped with their lives. The owner of the building, Mr. O.P. Weed, ran from his property, with only his clothing in hand. Thirty-eight horses, wild and crazed with fear died in the blaze, too confused to move. The frame building next door ignited.

One by one, every structure on the West side of Main Street began to burn. The north wind arose and fanned the flames along Second Street to Broadway. When it became apparent that nothing on the block could be saved, the firefighters turned their attention to protecting the block from Second to First Streets. Every roof and wooden awning was dotted with men passing buckets full of water hand to hand and back down the line empty. Citizens formed lines to hand goods out of the threatened shops and homes. Each person worked far into the morning to halt the progression of the flames.

In late March 1975, a huge fire burst into flames through Toad Hall at Broadway and 3rd Streets.

Captain David Main poses enthusiastically by a mural of a firefighter that was painted by local artist, Scott Teeple.

Ty Barbour

Our *Firefighters*

Chico ER

A common dream of many children is to one day become a firefighter.

Ty Barbour

Chico ER

After many meetings in the City Council chambers it was decided that parking meters were to be installed in down-town Chico. The meters were placed into action in December 1946. The penalties were announced as a $1.00 fine per violation if paid within 24 hours after the issuance of the citation. After 24 hours, the penalty was a $10.00 fine or two days in the county jail.

The term "Meter Maid" and "Brownie" have been replaced by "Traffic Enforcement Agent." The new term makes sense for two reasons: (1) they now wear black, and (2) there are men as well as women, and they write other tickets besides meter violations.

Marge had a brief television stint when she starred in a Burger King commercial during the 1980s. In fact, people called her from all over the United States to say they knew the commercial was made in Chico because they recognized the famous meter maid!

Ten businesses were gutted by the inferno and others were ruined by water when it was finally extinguished. Especially heart wrenching was the destruction of the pet shop that had been home to many small animals. Though firefighters diligently tried to save them, most were lost due to smoke inhalation.

An estimated $125,000 was reported for building damage, and another $75,000 in damages for the business contents. Fortunately the strong brick structure survived and was slowly able to open its doors to downtown again. Today we know the historic site as The Phoenix Building, it is owned by Morehead family members, and quite a hub for downtowners. Inside are cafes, a yogurt shop, and a whimsical gift shop that is filled with fun items.

In addition to the incidents mentioned above, the tragedy of fire has greatly impacted the history and the architectural make-up of Chico in numerous instances. The burning and rebuilding of numerous Chico landmarks such as the Majestic Theater, the Diamond Hotel and both Chico High School and Normal School (Chico State University) are vivid examples of fire's influence on our town.

With the advent of full-time firefighters came a much more efficient organization. During the 1970s, women began to enter the workforce as fulltime firefighters. The primary purpose of a fire department is to prevent the loss of lives and property. Today, a firefighter's job is far more diverse and training includes a great deal more than just putting out fires.

Marge the Meter Maid

This bright and witty, angular faced lady with the "big" hair-do, is Marge Saadoon. She is one of the most memorable Chico faces of all time. She worked as the

Ty Barbour, ER

meter maid in downtown Chico, writing tickets for 36 years. One can't fathom how many tickets she wrote during that time! She was adored by many, and disliked by even more because she took her job very seriously and did it extremely well. Some rogues thought that she looked like the wicked witch and would hum the song from "The Wizard of Oz" as she passed by. She hated to be con-fronted by violators, and would usually ignore any of their antics. At times, this would only aggravate people even more!

The woman behind the uniform and ticket book is originally from San Francisco and is a kind and generous human being. Marge came to Chico to go to college, left briefly, then came back to stay. She has lived here for over 42 years. A talented singer, she loves music, and is very active in her church.

Oser's

Downtown, on the corner of Third and Main Streets was M. Oser and Company. Morris Oser and Wolf Jacobs opened this grand store in 1878. It was quite chic for the time period in Chico. Ladies would travel from all over Butte County to shop at Oser's. There was not a hitching rack in front for horses and buggies; instead, Mr. Oser was known to personally come out front to help the ladies from their carriages.

The store was renovated during the late 1960s, adding the dramatic double staircase that is still in the building today. The cascading staircase was often used as a stage for fashion shows. During the late 1970s, a statuesque young Chicoan, Angie Kuhl (Worley) who was an incredibly talented manikin model, was hired to model fashionable clothes during special events at the store. She was amazing to watch, as she could stand motionless for what seemed like hours in the position of a manikin. Many people did not realize that she was a live human being and would become quite startled if she gave them a wink. If you were lucky, you could catch her move into a different pose. It was a favorite pastime for local rascals, such as the author's father, to tell Angie jokes to try and get her to crack a smile.

Long before chain department stores and mini-malls existed in Chico, Oser's was considered the only upscale department store in the area. Many young women in Chico were fitted for their first bra on the second floor of the store.

Photos courtesy Angie Worley

Oser's **SALE!** On your mark, get set, GO!

Oser's sales were marked on all of the ladies' calendars in Chico. There was always a crowd out front waiting for the store to open its doors. It was not uncommon for many of the overzealous shoppers to get downright pushy over sale items.

Bras and underwear were not nearly as much of a fashion statement as they are today. It was Oser's who stocked an extensive selection. They were sorted by size and color, then placed neatly in clear containers and shelved. Purchasing a bra was almost like viewing a fine piece of jewelry. The saleswoman would carefully select a bra and show it to the perspective buyer to see if they were interested in trying it on. If the patron was interested, the sales associate would measure the woman before the formal fitting in the dressing room. Mothers felt comfortable bringing their daughters to Oser's. This process took place well into the late 1970s.

Living manikins, Angie Kuhl and Josh Strong

It's impossible to write about Oser's and not mention Chicoan Ted Meriam, long-time Oser's sales associate who later became the store President. A lifelong Chicoan, he additionally served as Chico's mayor. He was a respected historian on Butte County. Meriam Library at Chico State University was renamed in honor of the Meriam Family in 1982.

In 1986 Oser's closed and later Bradley's Department Store opened in the same location. It was similar to Oser's, but never quite the same. The site was home to Sports LTD for 12 years. (They re-located to the Mangrove Plaza.) It currently houses an antique store.

O ♥ CHICO

JAN California

CA 2005
Y 6547510

Already well over a century old, Chico, California has demonstrated its worth to homegrown Chicoans and masses of college students. Many "transplants" have moved here from larger cities, making Chico their hometown. For countless, Chico has been a vital part of their family heritage. As we become more and more aware of the value— the need—for an offering of a comfortable lifestyle and culture in the modern world of ever-increasing industry, technology, and international political stress, Chico is an inviting place to call home.

In 1864 Chico had 500 residents. In 1900 the little town had an impressive 2500 residents. Today, the metropolitan area of Chico has 100,0000 people in its population.

Chico's treasures lie all around waiting to be noticed. Some are obvious, such as Bidwell Park, the university, and downtown. But others, such as interesting, benevolent people, talented artists, and wildlife galore, are waiting to be noticed and appreciated by many.

These, and many, many more, are the treasures that lie in store for those who take the time to look and to savor, My Hometown Chico.

Ty Barbour. ER

CHICOAN
MY HEART'S IN CHICO

The "next generation," for whom Chico is established, enjoying their hometown.

"There's *no place like home and* you don't have to go anywhere *to get there.*" —Andy Rooney

GOOD OLD CHICO

Marcia Wilhite

About the Author

Marcia Myers Wilhite is truly a local Chico girl. She was born at Enloe Hospital on one of Chico's notorious hot summer days in July, practically grew up on the Chico State campus, where her dad taught anthropology for 38 years, and has worked and lived in Chico her entire 40 years of life.

The mother of two energetic boys, ages 5 and 10, Marcia is also a step-mom to 3 college students who were raised in Chico. Her husband, Charlie, a bay area transplant, fell quickly in love with her hometown.

As many Chicoans, Marcia loves to spend time in Bidwell Park. Whether it's playing with her boys at Caper Acres, walking, running or exploring the depths of Upper Park with a good friend, or attending park-related events, Marcia is there. If not at the park, she often may be seen in downtown Chico with her wolf-dog, "Buddy Love," or sipping coffee before work with friends.

Gardening in Chico's rich soil is just one of her many passions. Cooking for her family and friends is something she does with great enthusiasm. She is an avid reader and loves to spend time in local bookstores. With photography being her hobby since she was a child, and always having been fascinated by the history and culture of Chico, Marcia felt compelled to publish her first book about Chico in 2003.

My Hometown Chico, published in 2003, sold out its first printing within one month's time. It is currently available in its second printing.

Ty Barbour

Ty was born and raised in Mill Valley, California. A 5th generation Californian, like many 18-year-olds, he came to Chico to go to college, and never left. While at Chico State, he met his future wife and they decided to make Chico their home. They have been married for 25 years and have three children.

Ty has worked for the Chico Enterprise Record for 28 years. His photographs are sensitive and insightful, connecting Chicoans to what is truly happening in the area. Not one to personally ever boast about his obvious talent as a photographer, Ty's work is phenomenal. He always gets the picture, no matter how difficult the conditions. In his infrequent time-off, Ty can be found boating on the Sacramento River. Ty's work is also shown in Marcia Wilhite's first book, *My Hometown Chico*.

Bibliography

Association for Northern California
Records and Research
Tales from "Old Hutch"
Chico, CA: 1990

Boze, M. Jeanne
The Nature of Bidwell Park
Paradise, CA: 1991

Chico Enterprise Record
Archives

Field, Ann
Scoble, Gretchen
The Meaning of Flowers
San Francisco, California: 1998

Gillis, Michael J.
Magliari, Michael F.
John Bidwell and California
The Life and Writings of a Pioneer
Spokane, Washington: 2003

Goni, Mary Compton
Mary Remembers
Chico, CA: 1990

Heizer, Robert
Kroeber, Theodora
Ishi the Last Yahi
Berkeley, California: 1979

Mansfield, George
History of Butte County
Los Angeles, CA: 1918

McGie, Joseph
History of Butte County
Chico, CA: 1956

Starn, Owen
Ishi's Brain
New York, New York: 2004

Wells and Chambers
Butte County, California
San Francisco, CA: 1882

Colophon

Photography: **Ty Barbour, Marcia Wilhite**

Graphic Design: **Connie Nixon**

Copy Editor: **Charlie Wilhite**